SPECTRUM®

Enrichment Math

Grade 8

Spectrum®
an imprint of Carson-Dellosa Publishing LLC
Greensboro, NC

Spectrum® is an imprint of Carson-Dellosa Publishing.

Printed in the United States of America. All rights reserved. Except as permitted under the United States Copyright Act, no part of this publication may be reproduced or distributed in any form or by any means, or stored in a database or retrieval system, without prior written permission from the publisher, unless otherwise indicated. Spectrum® is an imprint of Carson-Dellosa Publishing. © 2011 Carson-Dellosa Publishing.

Send all inquiries to:
Carson-Dellosa Publishing
P.O. Box 35665
Greensboro, NC 27425 USA

Printed in the USA   ISBN 978-0-7696-6338-8

02-031127811

Table of Contents Grade 8

Table of Contents, continued

Check What You Know

Whole Numbers, Decimals, and Fractions

Read the problem carefully and solve. Show your work under each question.

The Ortiz and Johnson families decide to go on a summer vacation together.

1. On three consecutive days, the families drove their cars 450 miles, 325 miles, and 236 miles. How many total miles did they drive on those days?

   ___1011___ miles

2. Along the highway, the children see a sign stating that Old Towne is $36\frac{1}{3}$ miles away and Bridgeway is $52\frac{1}{4}$ miles away. How far is it from Old Towne to Bridgeway?

   ___15 $\frac{11}{12}$___ miles

3. On the second day of the trip, the families go to an amusement park. They purchase 4 adult tickets for $49.99 each and 8 student tickets for $31 each. How much money do they get back if they pay with five $100 bills?

   ___$52.04___

4. After $2\frac{1}{2}$ days, the Johnsons had used $2\frac{2}{3}$ tanks of gas. How many tanks of gas were they using per day?

   ___1$\frac{1}{15}$___ tanks of gas

5. The Ortiz children were each given $20 spending money. By the end of day two, Joe had spent $\frac{7}{8}$ of his money, Lila had spent $\frac{3}{4}$ of her money, and Anton had spent $\frac{3}{5}$ of his money. How much money did the Ortiz children spend altogether?

   ___$44.50___

6. The Johnson's car averages 30 miles per gallon of gas. How many gallons of gas did they use on this trip?

   ___33.7___ gallons of gas

Lesson 1.1 Addition

Read the problem carefully and solve. Show your work under each question.

The superintendent of schools of a large city is gathering data to plan the school budget. The city has three districts. Each district has an elementary, middle or intermediate school, a high school, and a charter school.

Helpful Hint

Line up the numbers by place value when adding numbers with a different number of digits.

1. South High has 1,759 students. South Middle school has 2,395 students. South Charter has 658 students and South Elementary has 1,953 students. How many students are enrolled in schools in the southern part of the city?

    ___6765___ students

2. East High has 1,385 students. East Intermediate has 1,272 students. East Charter has 167 students and East Elementary has 124 students. How many students are enrolled in the schools in the eastern part of the city?

    ___2948___ students

3. West Elementary has 94 students. West Charter has 711 students. West High has 1,208 students and West Middle has 1,415 students. How many students are enrolled in school in the western part of the city?

    ___3428___ students

4. How many students attend charter schools in the city?

    ___1536___ students

5. How many students are enrolled in high schools in the city?

    ___4352___ students

Lesson 1.2 Subtraction

Read the problem carefully and solve. Show your work under each question.

Last year's fan attendance for a baseball team's home games is listed by month as follows: April, 315,950 fans; May, 334,553 fans; June, 381,055 fans; July, 229,607 fans; August, 346,932 fans; and September, 240,922 fans.

Helpful Hint

When subtracting, start with the ones digit. Rename 1 ten as 10 ones when necessary.

1. What is the difference between the attendance in April and the attendance in September?

   _75028_ fans

2. How many more fans attended games in June than attended in August?

   _34123_ fans

3. What is the difference in the number of fans that attended games in May than fans who attended games in July?

   _104946_ fans

4. What is the difference in the number of fans who attended games in June, July, and August and fans who attended games in April, May, and September?

   _66169_ fans

5. The team played three home games in October. If the total attendance for the year was 1,907,163, how many fans attended games in October?

   _58144_ fans

Lesson 1.3 Multiplication

Read the problem carefully and solve. Show your work under each question.

Eagle Middle School is holding a read-a-thon to raise money for victims of an earthquake. Approved books include a sports book that has 823 pages, a non-fiction book that has 1,204 pages, a fiction book that has 2,059 pages, and a book of short stories that has 1,673 pages.

Helpful Hint

To multiply by a two-digit number, first multiply the top number by each of the digits in the bottom number. Then, add the two products to find the solution.

1. Of the 32 students in Homeroom A, 7 students chose to read the non-fiction book, 19 students chose to read the sports books, and 6 students chose to read the fiction book. How many pages will the students in Homeroom A read?

    __36419__ pages

2. The teacher in Homeroom B assigned the book of short stories to the entire class of 28 students. How many pages in total did the students in Homeroom B read?

    __46844__ pages

3. The 12 girls in Homeroom C each read the non-fiction book and the 14 boys read the sports book. How many pages in total did the students in Homeroom C read?

    __25970__ pages

4. The 47 members of the eighth-grade Literary Club decide to form their own team. These students all agreed to read the fiction book. How many total pages did the Literary Club members read?

    __96773__ pages

5. The 16 boys in Homeroom D decided to read the sports book and the fiction book. The 19 girls in Homeroom D decided to read the fiction book and the short story book. How many pages in total did the students in Homeroom D read?

    __117,020__ pages

Lesson 1.4 Division

Read the problem carefully and solve. Show your work under each question.

A bottled water company packages 12-ounce water bottles. Packages are sold in groups of 6, 12, or cases of 24 bottles.

> **Helpful Hint**
>
> When dividing, make sure the numbers are positioned correctly with each step.

1. During the morning shift, 1,252 bottles were packed in cases of 24 bottles. How many full cases were packed? How many bottles were remaining?

   ___52___ cases

   ___4___ bottles remaining

2. During the afternoon shift, workers were asked to make packages of 12 bottles from a total of 2,568 bottles. How many packages of 12 bottles were made? How many bottles were remaining?

   ___214___ packages of 12

   ___0___ bottles remaining

3. The overnight shift packaged 5,780 bottles in groups of six bottles. How many packages were made? How many bottles were remaining?

   ___963___ packages

   ___2___ bottles remaining

4. The company received an order for 31,620 bottles of water. The boss would like to send the least number of packages without having any bottles left over. How many bottles should be in each package? How many packages will there be in total?

   ___12___ bottles in a package

   ___2635___ packages

5. An order was received for 10,000 bottles. The customer asked that 6,000 bottles be packaged in cases of 24 and that the remainder be packaged in groups of 6. How many cases of 24 bottles were made? How many packages of 6 bottles were made? How many, if any, bottles were remaining?

   ___250___ cases of 24

   ___666___ packages of 6

   ___4___ bottles remaining

Lesson 1.5 Adding and Subtracting Decimals

Read the problem carefully and solve. Show your work under each question.

Darius has $4,375 in his savings account. Chris has $5,749.60 in his savings account.

> **Helpful Hint**
>
> Remember to line up the decimal points when adding and subtracting decimals.

1. How much money do Darius and Chris have together in their savings accounts?

$10124.6

2. What is the difference between what Chris has saved and what Darius has saved?

$1374.6

3. Darius withdraws $225 to pay for a school trip. How much money is left in his account?

$4150

4. Chris withdraws $249.99 to buy a new cell phone. How much money is left in his account?

$5399.61

5. What is the difference between what Chris and Darius have remaining in their savings accounts?

$1249.61

Lesson 1.6 Multiplying Decimals

Read the problem carefully and solve. Show your work under each question.

Sara agrees to go grocery shopping to help her mom get ready for a cookout they are hosting. Some of the items on Sara's list include ground beef, rolls, potato salad, and bottled water.

Helpful Hint

There are no U.S. coins worth less than $0.01, so when finding the cost of an item, round your answer to the nearest hundredth of a dollar.

1. Sara chooses a package of ground beef that weighs 3.5 pounds and costs $2.49 a pound. How much does she pay for the ground beef?

   $8.72

2. At the deli counter, Sara gets 5 pounds of potato salad for $1.99 per pound and 3 packages of rolls for $1.25 per package. How much money does Sara spend at the deli counter?

   $13.70

3. Sara finds that a 24-pack of bottled water is on sale for $3.99 and buys 3 packs. How much does Sara spend on bottled water?

   $11.97

4. Sara decides that it would be nice to serve a green salad at the cookout. She gets 2.25 pounds of tomatoes for $1.88 per pound, a head of lettuce for $1.89, 1.75 pounds of carrots for $1.59 per pound, and 1.5 pounds of broccoli for $1.69 a pound. How much does Sara spend altogether on vegetables?

   $11.44

5. Sara decides to buy 2 pounds of strawberries for $2.99 per pound and 3 pounds of blueberries for $1.88 per pound. How much does Sara spend on fruit?

   $11.62

Lesson 1.7 Dividing Decimals

Read the problem carefully and solve. Show your work under each question.

Mr. Benson is making plans for the eighth-grade field trip to the local science museum. He will collect admission fees and recruit adult chaperones. Students and adults will have the option to either bring their lunches or buy their lunches at the museum.

Helpful Hint

When working with decimals in money, be sure to show your answer to the hundredths place.

No: $5.6   Yes: $5.60

Add zero to show 60 cents.

---

1. Mr. Benson collects a total $3,116.00 from the students for admission to the museum. If each student ticket costs $20.50, how many students will go on the field trip?

   __152__ students

2. Each chaperone's ticket to the museum costs $24.50. Mr. Benson collects $367.50 from the chaperones. How many chaperones will go on the field trip?

   __15__ chaperones

3. Five friends have lunch at the museum café. Their bill comes to a total of $62.25. The friends decide to split the bill evenly. How much will each student pay?

   __$12.45__

4. A group of 65 students decides to attend a special program at the museum. They pay a total of $487.50 for admission to the program. What is the cost for each student to attend the program?

   __$7.50__

5. Mr. Benson and the chaperones decided to treat the students to frozen yogurt cones on the way home. The total bill is $380.00. If the 15 chaperones and Mr. Benson split the bill evenly, how much does each adult pay?

   __$23.75__

Lesson 1.8 Reducing to Simplest Form

Read the problem carefully and solve. Show your work under each question.

A kindergarten teacher has a bucket of 51 crayons and another bucket of 5 red pencils, 14 blue pencils, and 6 green pencils. The bucket of crayons contains 19 red crayons, 17 blue crayons, 9 green crayons and 6 yellow crayons.

Helpful Hint

Remember to find the **greatest common factor (GCF)** to reduce fractions to their simplest form. The **greatest common factor** is the largest number that can evenly divide into two or more numbers.

1. What is the fraction of red pencils to the total number of pencils written in simplest form?

    1/5

2. What is the fraction of blue crayons to the total number of crayons written in simplest form?

    1/3

3. What is the fraction of green crayons to the total number of crayons written in simplest form?

    3/17

4. The teacher places the crayons and pencils in one bucket. What is the fraction of yellow crayons and green pencils written in simplest form?

    3/19

5. Pencils come in boxes of 6. The number of boxes of blue pencils in the bucket can be represented by the mixed numeral $2\frac{2}{6}$. What is the number of boxes in simplest form?

    2 1/3

NAME _____

Lesson 1.9 Renaming Fractions and Mixed Numbers

Read the problem carefully and solve. Show your work under each question.

Khalil is making his own board game. He needs to purchase special cardboard to make the cards for the game. The cardboard comes in the following widths: $\frac{15}{4}$ inches, $\frac{36}{8}$ inches, $\frac{20}{16}$ inches, $6\frac{5}{7}$ inches, and $8\frac{1}{2}$ inches.

Helpful Hint

A mixed numeral is not in simplest form if:
- the fraction is not reduced
- the fraction is improper

1. Khalil needs to convert the fraction $\frac{15}{4}$ to a mixed numeral in simplest form. What is this fraction as a mixed numeral in simplest form?

    _____ $3\frac{3}{4}$ _____

2. Change the width $\frac{36}{8}$ inches to a mixed numeral in simplest form.

    _____ $4\frac{1}{2}$ _____ inches

3. Change the width $\frac{20}{16}$ inches to a mixed numeral in simplest form.

    _____ $1\frac{1}{4}$ _____ inches

4. Khalil changes the width $6\frac{5}{7}$ inches into an improper fraction. What is $6\frac{5}{7}$ as an improper fraction?

    _____ $47/7$ _____ inches

5. Change the width $8\frac{1}{2}$ inches into an improper fraction.

    _____ $17/2$ _____ inches

Grade 8
10

Lesson 1.9
Renaming Fractions and Mixed Numbers

Lesson 1.10 Adding and Subtracting Fractions and Mixed Numerals

Read the problem carefully and solve. Show your work under each question.

Shannon is decorating her new bedroom. She is making a bedspread and curtains from two different fabrics, one solid blue and one with a flower pattern.

> **Helpful Hint**
>
> Remember to rename fractions with the least common denominator and change to simplest form when the fractions have different denominators.

1. Shannon needs $2\frac{2}{5}$ yards of the solid fabric for the bedspread and $2\frac{7}{8}$ yards of the solid fabric for the curtains. How much solid fabric does Shannon need for this project?

_____ $5\,{}^{11}\!/_{40}$ _____ yards

2. Shannon needs $2\frac{1}{3}$ yards of the patterned fabric for the bedspread and $2\frac{7}{8}$ yards of the patterned fabric for the curtains. How much patterned fabric does Shannon need for this project?

_____ $5\,{}^{5}\!/_{24}$ _____ yards

3. Shannon needs $1\frac{1}{2}$ yards of curtain rod for one curtain and $9\frac{1}{4}$ yards of curtain rod for another curtain. How many yards of curtain rod does Shannon need for both curtains?

_____ $10\,{}^{3}\!/_{4}$ _____ yards

4. Shannon needs a total of 6 yards of lining fabric for the curtains. She already has $2\frac{7}{12}$ yards of lining fabric. How much more lining fabric does she need?

_____ $3\,{}^{5}\!/_{12}$ _____ yards

5. Shannon's mother gives her $2\frac{1}{4}$ yards of blue solid fabric. How much blue solid fabric does she still need to purchase?

_____ $3\,{}^{1}\!/_{40}$ _____ yards

Lesson 1.11 Multiplying Fractions and Mixed Numerals

Read the problem carefully and solve. Show your work under each question.

Cadence is making cookies and muffins for a bake sale.

Helpful Hint

Remember to rename each mixed numeral as an improper fraction before multiplying. Be sure to simplify all fractions.

1. The cookie recipe calls for $1\frac{3}{4}$ cups of flour for 1 batch of muffins. How much flour does Cadence need if she wants to make $2\frac{1}{2}$ batches of muffins?

_____4 3/8_____ cups

2. The cookie recipe calls for $\frac{3}{4}$ cup of light brown sugar. How much brown sugar is needed for $2\frac{1}{2}$ batches?

_____1 7/8_____ cups

3. Cadence adds $1\frac{1}{2}$ cups of chocolate bits per batch of cookies. How many cups of chocolate bits does she need for $2\frac{1}{2}$ batches?

_____3 3/4_____ cups

4. The muffin recipe calls for $\frac{1}{3}$ cup of oatmeal. How many cups of oatmeal does Cadence need if she wants to make $3\frac{1}{4}$ batches?

_____1 1/12_____ cups

5. There is $\frac{1}{4}$ teaspoon of salt in each batch of one type of cookie. How much salt is needed for $3\frac{1}{4}$ batches?

_____13/16_____ teaspoons

Lesson 1.12 Dividing Fractions and Mixed Numerals

Read the problem carefully and solve. Show your work under each question.

Caleb has 5 pieces of scrap wood he will use to make picture frames. The first piece of wood is $2\frac{1}{2}$ yards long. The second piece of wood is $\frac{3}{4}$ yard long. The third piece of wood is $1\frac{1}{8}$ yards long. The fourth piece of wood is $5\frac{1}{5}$ yards long. The fifth piece of wood is $4\frac{8}{10}$ yards long.

Helpful Hint

To divide mixed numerals:

- rename each mixed numeral as an improper fraction
- multiply by the reciprocal of the divisor
- simplify all fractions

1. How many $\frac{1}{4}$-yard pieces can Caleb cut from the first piece of wood?

_____10_____ pieces

2. How many $\frac{3}{16}$-yard pieces can Caleb cut from the second piece of wood?

_____4_____ pieces

3. How many $\frac{3}{16}$-yard pieces can Caleb cut from the third piece of wood?

_____6_____ pieces

4. How many $1\frac{3}{10}$-yard pieces can Caleb cut from the fourth piece of wood?

_____4_____ pieces

5. How many $\frac{4}{5}$-yard pieces can Caleb cut from the fifth piece of wood?

_____6_____ pieces

Check What You Learned

Whole Numbers, Decimals, and Fractions

Read the problem carefully and solve. Show your work under each question.

The eighth-grade teachers are making plans for their end-of-year field day. The number of students in each homeroom is: Mr. Chung's, 25 students; Mrs. Bertrand's, 27 students; Mr. Gupta's, 32 students; and Mrs. Ross's, 26 students.

1. School policy requires that one chaperone per 10 students is required at the field day. How many chaperones are needed?

_____11_____ chaperones

2. There will be team events in which $\frac{7}{10}$ of the total number of students will participate. How many students will participate in team events?

_____77_____ students

3. Each homeroom will contribute to purchasing new sporting equipment for the field day. The equipment costs $356.84. If the cost is split evenly between the 4 homerooms, how much will each homeroom contribute?

$89.21

4. Mrs. Bertrand buys 5 yards of ribbon to make awards for the students. She cuts the ribbon into $\frac{1}{8}$-yard pieces. How many pieces will she have?

_____40_____ pieces

5. A group of parents purchased 35 pizzas for the field day. Of the 35 pizzas, 0.6 are cheese pizzas. How many cheese pizzas were purchased?

_____21_____ cheese pizzas

6. During the running events, 15 students ran 0.25 miles, 12 students ran 0.3 miles, and 25 students ran 0.5 miles. How many total miles did these students run?

_____19.85_____ miles

Check What You Know

Ratio and Proportion

Read the problem carefully and solve. Show your work under each question.

After school, Chang plans to do his homework, take a walk, and cook dinner.

---

1. Chang can solve 4 math problems in 10 minutes. How long will it take him to solve 30 problems?

___75___ minutes

2. Chang reads 18 pages of his history book in 20 minutes. How many pages can he read in 1 hour?

___54___ pages

3. Chang wrote a 928-word essay. He types 32 words per minute. How long will it take him to type his paper?

___29___ minutes

4. It takes Chang 45 minutes to walk 3 miles. How many miles can he walk in 2 hours?

___8___ miles

5. Chang is making biscuits to have with dinner. If 2 tablespoons of baking powder are needed to make 16 biscuits, how many biscuits can Chang make with 5 tablespoons of baking powder?

___40___ biscuits

6. Two batches of biscuit batter require 4 cups of flour. Chang will make 3 batches. How much flour does he need?

___6___ cups

Lesson 2.1 Ratio and Proportion

Read the problem carefully and solve. Show your work under each question.

Natasha and Alexis each have a bag of marbles and a bag of coins.

Helpful Hint

Use cross multiplication to check if two ratios form a proportion.

1. One fourth of Natalie's marbles are green. Alexis has 15 green marbles out of a total of 64 marbles in her bag. Is the ratio of green marbles to the total amount the same for both bags of marbles?

_____ No _____

2. Natalie has 54 blue marbles out of a total of 144 marbles. In Alexis's bag of marbles, $\frac{3}{8}$ of the marbles are blue. Is the ratio of blue marbles to the total number of marbles the same for both bags?

_____ Yes _____

3. Natalie has 27 red marbles out of a total of 144 marbles. Alexis has 12 red marbles out of a total of 64 marbles. Do the ratios of red marbles to the total numbers in each bag form a proportion?

_____ Yes _____

4. Natalie counts 45 pennies out of a total of 85 coins. Alexis has 35 pennies out of a total of 75 coins. Is the ratio of pennies to the total number of coins the same for both bags?

_____ No _____

5. Natalie's bag of coins has 17 quarters out of a total of 85 coins. Alexis has 15 quarters out of a total of 75 coins. Do the ratios of quarters to the total number of coins in each bag form a proportion?

_____ Yes _____

Lesson 2.2 Solving Proportion Equations

Read the problem carefully and solve. Show your work under each question.

A group of students is helping to decorate flowerbeds for a local senior center. They will paint rocks different colors to place in the flowerbeds. After they paint the rocks, the children will be served juice and trail mix.

Helpful Hint

When setting up a proportion, be sure to align the units.

No: $\dfrac{miles}{hours} = \dfrac{hours}{miles}$ Yes: $\dfrac{miles}{hours} = \dfrac{miles}{hours}$

1. Jessica can paint 12 rocks in 8 minutes. How many rocks can she paint in 48 minutes?

   ___72___ rocks

2. Ronnie can paint 8 rocks in 5 minutes. How long will it take him to paint 54 rocks?

   ___34___ minutes

3. A group of volunteers is filling baskets to give to the students. It takes 10 minutes to fill 3 baskets. How long will it take to fill 75 baskets?

   ___250___ minutes

4. It takes 6 students to decorate 20 flowerbeds. How many students are needed to decorate 30 flowerbeds?

   ___9___ students

5. Thirty-six ounces of juice will serve 6 students. How many children can be served with 162 ounces?

   ___27___ children

Check What You Learned

Ratio and Proportion

Read the problem carefully and solve. Show your work under each question.

Tanesha is making scrapbook albums to sell at a crafts fair. She will use a number of supplies including airbrush markers, stickers, card stock and sheet protectors.

1. Tanesha can make 3 scrapbook albums in 2 hours. How long will it take her to make 105 albums?

   ___4200___ minutes

2. Seven pieces of cardstock sell for $3. Tanesha spends $57 on cardstock. How many pieces of cardstock does Tanesha buy?

   ___133___ pieces of cardstock

3. Alphabet cutouts come in packages of 6 sheets for $8. How much does Tanesha spend on alphabet cutouts if she needs 72 sheets?

   ___$96___

4. Tanesha spends $84 on markers. The markers are priced at 4 for $14. How many markers does Tanesha purchase?

   ___24___ markers

5. Five sheet protectors cost $7. If Tanesha purchases 115 sheet protectors, how much does Tanesha spend on sheet protectors?

   ___$161___

6. Patterned sheets cost $0.50 each or packages of 60 for $19.99. If Tanesha needs 92 sheets, how much will she save if she buys 2 packages instead of paying individually for the sheets?

   ___$6.02___

Check What You Know

Percents and Interest

Read the problem carefully and solve. Show your work under each question.

Nadia manages a vehicle dealership. She is in charge of the inventory and the finances.

1. Nadia finds that 35% of the vehicles in the lot are trucks. What is this percent as a decimal and as a fraction in simplest form?

___0.35___ and ___7/20___

2. Of the 220 cars in the lot, 15% are red. How many red cars are there?

___33___ red cars

3. If 495 of the 1,650 vehicles are trucks, what percent of the vehicles are trucks?

___30%___

4. Forty-two blue vans make up 40% of the total number of vans. How many vans are there in all?

___105___ vans

5. Nadia took out a loan of $12,000 with simple interest of 4% to make improvements at the dealership. How much interest does Nadia pay after 3 years?

___$1440___

6. Nadia put $2,340 from her salary in a savings account that earns 5% compounded quarterly. How much is in her account after 1 year? Round your answer to the nearest hundredth.

___$2459.22___

Lesson 3.1 Understanding Percents

Read the problem carefully and solve. Show your work under each question.

The students on the middle school math team won their last meet by scoring a record number of points.

Helpful Hint

Percent to fraction:

$30\% = 30 \times \frac{1}{100} = \frac{3}{100} = \frac{3}{10}$

Percent to decimal:

$15\% = 15 \times 0.01 = 0.15$

1. Julie scored 24% of the team's points. Express this percent as a decimal and fraction in simplest form.

   ___0.24___ and ___6/25___

2. Michael scored 9% of the team's points. Express this percent as a decimal and fraction in simplest form.

   ___0.09___ and ___9/100___

3. Together, Renee and Bobbi scored 36% of the team's points. Express this percent as a decimal and fraction in simplest form.

   ___0.36___ and ___9/25___

4. The math team's score was 105% higher than the winner's score from the last meet. Express this percent as a decimal and fraction in simplest form.

   ___1.05___ or ___1 1/20___

5. The math team members expect to improve their scores by 125% at the next meet. Express this percent as a decimal and fraction in simplest form.

   ___1.25___ or ___1 1/4___

Lesson 3.2 Percent to Fraction and Fraction to Percent

Read the problem carefully and solve. Show your work under each question.

Kevin is creating a budget to keep track of how he spends his money each week.

> **Helpful Hint**
>
> Fraction to percent:
>
> $\frac{1}{4} = \frac{n}{100}$ $\qquad$ $\frac{1}{4} \times \frac{25}{25} = \frac{25}{100} = 25\%$

1. Kevin spends 15% of his budget on transportation. What is this number as a fraction in simplest form?

$\underline{\quad 3/20 \quad}$

2. Kevin spends $\frac{1}{8}$ of his money on snacks. What percent of Kevin's budget is spent on snacks?

$\underline{\quad 12.5\% \quad}$

3. Guitar lessons takes up $\frac{2}{5}$ of the budget. What percent of the budget is used for guitar lessons?

$\underline{\quad 40\% \quad}$

4. Kevin expects his weekly budget next year to be 125% of what it is now. What is this percent shown as a mixed numeral?

$\underline{\quad 1\frac{1}{4} \quad}$

5. Kevin uses $5\frac{1}{2}\%$ of his money for entertainment. What is this percent as a fraction in simplest form?

$\underline{\quad {}^{11}/_{200} \quad}$

Lesson 3.3 Percent to Decimal and Decimal to Percent

Read the problem carefully and solve. Show your work under each question.

Mr. Lawson coaches the Eagles baseball team. He is studying the statistics of his players to determine changes he will make for the next game.

Helpful Hint

Decimal to percent:

$$0.27 \times \frac{0.27}{1} = \frac{0.27 \times 100}{100} = 27\%$$

1. The Eagles' first baseman has a batting average of 0.274. What is this decimal number as a percent?

  27.4%

2. Junior plays second base and gets a hit 58.7% of the time when there is someone on base. What is this percent as a decimal?

  0.587

3. The Eagles' best pitcher has a winning percentage of 65.2%. What is this percent as a decimal?

  0.652

4. Mr. Lawson has a winning percentage of 63%. What is this percent as a decimal?

  0.63

5. The three outfielders get on base at a rate represented by the decimal 0.365. What is this decimal as a percent?

  36.5%

Lesson 3.4 Finding Percent

Read the problem carefully and solve. Show your work under each question.

Colby conducted a survey. He asked 125 eighth graders what type of music was their favorite.

Helpful Hint

Remember to change the % to either a fraction or a decimal when solving percent problems.

---

1. If 20% of the eighth graders said rap music is their favorite type of music, what is the total number of students who gave this response?

    _____25_____ students

2. If 28% of the students said rock is their favorite type of music, how many students is this?

    _____35_____ students

3. Ten of the 125 students like country music best. What percent of the eighth graders like country music best?

    _____8%_____

4. Classical music is the favorite music of 50 out of the 125 eighth graders. What percent of the students like classical music best?

    _____40%_____

5. A seventh-grade teacher decided to have her students take the same survey. She found that 7 students, or 35% of her students, prefer rock music. How many students are in this class?

    _____20_____ students

Lesson 3.5 Figuring Simple Interest

Read the problem carefully and solve. Show your work under each question.

Kayla works at a bank and approves home improvement loans. Loans are approved at simple interest for a variety of rates and time periods.

> **Helpful Hint**
>
> To find simple interest, use the formula:
>
> Interest = principal × rate × time
>
> Time is measured in years.

1. Rudy's loan for $450 was approved at a rate of 5% for 3 years. How much interest will he pay?

$67.50

2. Norman's loan for $6,990 was approved at $4\frac{1}{2}$% for 2 years. How much interest will he pay?

$329.10

3. Lin got a $8,100 loan for 4 years. She paid $2,106 in interest. What was the interest rate?

6.5%

4. Robert got a loan for $3\frac{1}{2}$ years. The interest rate was 7%. He paid $600.25 in interest. How much was the principal?

$2450

5. Jessica got a loan for $55,000. The interest rate was 8%. She paid $22,000 in interest. What was the length of the loan?

____5____ years

Lesson 3.6 Figuring Compound Interest

Read the problem carefully and solve. Show your work under each question.

Five students each won $500 in an academic competition. Each student put the $500 in a savings account.

Helpful Hint

To find compound interest, use the formula

$A = P(1 + \frac{r}{n})^{nt}$

In this formula, *P* is the principal, *r* is the interest rate, *n* is the number of times the interest is compounded annually, and *t* is the time in years.

$A = \$450(1 + \frac{0.05}{4})^{4 \times 1} = \$472.93$

3. Addie put her $500 in a savings account that earns 7% interest compounded quarterly. How much will be in the account after 1 year? Round your answer to the nearest hundredth.

_____

1. Melissa put her $500 in a savings account that earns 4% interest compounded annually. How much will be in the account after 3 years? Round your answer to the nearest hundredth.

$562.43

4. Brian put his $500 in a savings account that earns 6% interest compounded semi-annually. How much will be in the account after 2 years? Round your answer to the nearest hundredth.

_____

2. Gabe put his $500 in a savings account that earns $3\frac{1}{2}$% compounded monthly. How much will be in the account after 6 months? Round your answer to the nearest hundredth.

_____

5. Ryan put his $500 in a savings account that earns $5\frac{1}{4}$% compounded monthly. How much will be in the account after $\frac{1}{4}$ of a year? Round your answer to the nearest hundredth.

_____

Check What You Learned

Percents and Interest

Read the problem carefully and solve. Show your work under each question.

Mrs. Taylor is organizing her family's finances. The electric bill is $642.00 and the credit card bill is $576. She is also looking at Joanne's student loan of $10,000.

1. Mrs. Taylor finds that the family spent 14% of its budget on entertainment last month. What is this percent as a decimal and a fraction in simplest form?

0.14   7/50

2. The electric bill is $642.00. If the bill is paid early, Mrs. Taylor can take 10% off the bill. How much money will Mrs. Taylor save if she pays the bill early?

$64.20

3. The credit card bill is $576. If Mrs. Taylor pays $259.20, what percent of the bill does she pay?

45%

4. Mrs. Taylor bought a new microwave oven that was on sale for $450. This price is 75% of the original price. What was the original price of the microwave oven?

$600

5. Joanne's student loan of $10,000 has a simple interest rate of 6%. How much interest does she pay after 3 years?

$1800

6. The Taylor family put $200 in a savings account. The account earns $3\frac{1}{4}$% interest compounded semi-annually. How much interest will be in the account after 2 years? Round to the nearest hundredth.

$213.32

NAME ________________

Check What You Know

Customary Measurement

CHAPTER 4 PRETEST

Read the problem carefully and solve. Show your work under each question.

Jason loves to help his grandfather Edgar with all his various projects. The newest project involves installing and painting a new fence for the backyard. Jason will be working on one end of the fence.

1. The section of fence Jason will be working on is 21 feet 5 inches long. How many inches is this section of the fence?

   257 inches

2. Once the fence is installed, Jason uses 6 gallons 3 quarts of paint. How many quarts does Jason use?

   27 quarts

3. Each board of fencing weighs 7 pounds 4 ounces. How many ounces does each board weigh?

   116 ounces

4. Jason waits $\frac{3}{8}$ day for the paint to dry before applying a second coat. How many hours does Jason wait?

   9 hours

5. Jason has 3 pints 1 cup of paint left in his container. His grandfather adds 2 pints 1 cup to Jason's container. How many cups do they now have?

   12 cups

6. Edgar decided to add a second gate. He removes 2 yards 1 foot of fencing from his section of 13 yards. How much fencing is left?

   10 yards 2 feet

Lesson 4.1 Units of Length (inches, feet, yards, and miles)

Read the problem carefully and solve. Show your work under each question.

The eighth graders at Hamilton Middle School volunteer to help wrap gifts at the mall. The money they make will help defer the cost of their next field trip. Caitlyn volunteers to make all the bows of various sizes and colors.

Helpful Hint

1 foot (ft.) = 12 inches (in.)

1 yard (yd.) = 3 ft.

1 yd. = 36 in.

1 mile (mi.) = 5,280 ft.

1 mi. = 1,760 yd.

1. It takes 48 inches of blue ribbon to make 1 bow. How many bows can Caitlyn make with 12 feet of ribbon?

   _____ bows

2. Caitlyn has $4\frac{2}{3}$ yards of red ribbon. How many bows can she make if it takes 2 feet of ribbon to make each red bow?

   _____ bows

3. The red ribbon is $\frac{1}{12}$ yard wide. How many inches wide is the red ribbon?

   ____3____ inches

4. The table Caitlyn is working on is 6 feet 3 inches long. How many inches long is the table?

   _____ inches

5. Caitlyn walks 3,960 feet to the mall. What fraction of a mile does she walk?

   _____ mile

Lesson 4.2 Liquid Volume
(cups, pints, quarts, and gallons)

Read the problem carefully and solve. Show your work under each question.

Travis is helping to plan his sister's third birthday party. He suggests that they serve iced tea to the adults and milk and juice to the children. He also wants to have bottled water available.

Helpful Hint

1 pint (pt.) = 2 cups (c.)

1 quart (qt.) = 2 pt.

1 gallon (gal.) = 4 qt.

1. Travis makes 3 quarts of iced tea. How many pints is that?

_____ pints

2. Travis buys 2 quarts of orange juice. How many cups is that?

_____ cups

3. Two cases of water bottles contain 12 quarts. How many gallons of water are there?

_____ gallons

4. Travis decides to also make punch for the party. The punch recipe calls for $\frac{7}{8}$ quart of lemonade. How many cups is that?

_____ cups

5. Travis's mother has 3 cups of milk in the refrigerator. In order to have enough milk, she needs to buy 2 gallons 3 quarts. How many pints will she buy?

_____ pints

Lesson 4.3 Weight and Time (ounces, pounds, and tons)

Read the problem carefully and solve. Show your work under each question.

Mr. Marino is the foreman for a cereal packing company. He is in charge of two shifts per day. The first-shift workers run the machines that fill boxes with 14 ounces of cereal and the second-shift employees run the machines that fill boxes with 30 ounces of cereal.

Helpful Hint

16 ounces (oz.) = 1 pound (lb.)

2,000 lb. = 1 ton (T.)

60 seconds (sec.) = 1 minute (min.)

60 min. = 1 hour (hr.)

24 hr. = 1 day

1. During the first shift, one machine dispenses cereal into 24 boxes in 5 minutes. How many pounds of cereal are packaged?

_____21_____ pounds

2. The second-shift machines dispense $52\frac{1}{2}$ pounds of cereal each quarter hour. How many boxes do the machines fill each half hour?

_____56_____ boxes

3. Second-shift employees work 7 hours each day. How many minutes do they work each day?

_____420_____ minutes

4. Each employee takes 30 minutes for a lunch break. How many seconds are there in 30 minutes?

_____1800_____ seconds

5. A shipment of cereal boxes contains 7,000 pounds of cereal. How many tons does it contain?

_____3.5_____ tons

Lesson 4.4 Adding Measures
(length, liquid volume, weight, and time)

Read the problem carefully and solve. Show your work under each question.

Ty works at the pet store on Saturdays. Some of his responsibilities include stocking shelves, making the house blend of dog food, and filling the aquariums.

Helpful Hint

You can add measures, and then convert the units.

1 hr. 45 min.
+ 2 hr. 23 min.
68 min. = (1 hr.) 8 min.

4 hr. 8 min.

1. Ty mixes 5 pounds 10 ounces of Choice A dog food with 7 pounds 13 ounces of Choice B dog food to make a bag of House Blend. How much dog food is in the bag of House Blend?

   _____ pounds _____ ounces

2. Ty adds 10 gallons 3 quarts of water to 13 gallons 2 quarts of water in an aquarium. How much water is now in the aquarium?

   _____ gallons _____ quarts

3. A customer combines 2 pounds 12 ounces of yellow stones and 3 pounds 7 ounces of green stones for her aquarium. Ty places the stones in a bag. How much does the bag weigh?

   _____ pounds _____ ounces

4. Ty cuts two walking rope lengths for a customer. One length is 7 yards 1 foot and the other length is 6 yards 2 feet. What is the total length, in yards, of the two ropes?

   _____ yards

5. Ty works 2 hours 20 minutes before lunch, and 3 hours 45 minutes after. How long does Ty work?

   _____ hours _____ minutes

Lesson 4.5 Subtracting Measures
(length, liquid volume, weight, and time)

Read the problem carefully and solve. Show your work under each question.

The Girard family celebrates Mrs. Girard's work promotion with a special evening of dinner and activities. Mr. Girard serves a chicken dinner. After dinner, the family relaxes by playing board games.

Helpful Hint

You can subtract measures.

$$\begin{array}{r} \overset{2}{\cancel{3}} \text{ gal. } \cancel{1} \text{ qt.} \\ - 1 \text{ gal. } 2 \text{ qt.} \\ \hline 1 \text{ gal. } 3 \text{ qt.} \end{array}$$

1. Mr. Girard cooks 5 pounds of chicken. The family consumes 3 pounds 6 ounces. How much chicken was left?

    ___1___ pounds ___10___ ounces

2. The family drank 2 quarts and 1 pint of milk. They had 3 quarts at the beginning of the meal. How much milk is left?

    ___1___ pints

3. Mrs. Girard chooses "linear measurements" as a category during the game. Her question is "Subtract 2 yards 2 feet from 4 yards 1 foot." What is the correct answer in feet?

    ___5___ feet

4. Nicole chooses "time" as a category during the game. Her question is "What is the time difference between 5 minutes 15 seconds and 2 minutes 30 seconds?" What is the correct answer in minutes and seconds?

    ___2___ minutes ___45___ seconds

5. This special evening took up 4 hours and 15 minutes. The family played games for 2 hours and 45 minutes. How long did they spend at the dinner table?

    ___1___ hours ___30___ minutes

Check What You Learned

Customary Measurement

Read the problem carefully and solve. Show your work under each question.

The Nguyen family is visiting relatives in another state. They will first fly by airplane, and then rent a car to drive to their final destination.

---

1. During the flight, the plane travels at an altitude of 23,760 feet. How many miles is that?

_____ miles

$$\frac{2376}{8228} \quad \frac{1188}{264} \quad \frac{594}{132}$$

2. The rental car is filled with $23\frac{1}{4}$ gallons of gas. How many quarts is that?

_____ quarts

3. The total weight of the luggage on the flight is 4,338 pounds. What is the weight written in tons and pounds?

_____ tons _____ pounds

4. The flight was 3 hours 23 minutes long. How many minutes is that?

_____ minutes

5. Aidyn's suitcase weighs 32 pounds 10 ounces, and Hayden's suitcase weighs 47 pounds 9 ounces. How much do the two suitcases weigh together?

_____ pounds _____ ounces

6. The entire trip took 5 hours and 15 minutes. If the flight was 3 hours 23 minutes long, how long was the car ride?

_____ hour _____ minute

NAME _____

Check What You Know

Metric Measurements

Read the problem carefully and solve. Show your work under each question.

Students in the Science Club are working on their science projects for the science fair and competition. Hayley is studying plant growth. Dylan is building two different types of bridges to see which one can hold the most weight. Pedro is studying the effects of various disinfectants on bacteria.

1. At the beginning of the project, Hayley's plant is 3.12 centimeters tall. How many millimeters is this?

_____ millimeters

2. After the first week, Hayley's plant was 4.92 centimeters tall. By the end of week two, the plant was 5.3 centimeters tall. How much did the plant grow in meters between week one and week two?

_____ meter

3. Dylan uses an 11-kilogram weight to test the sturdiness of the bridges. How much is this weight in grams?

_____ grams

4. Dylan adds a 225-gram weight and a 1,250-gram weight to each bridge. How much total weight in kilograms did he add?

_____ kilograms

5. Pedro uses bleach for his experiment. The bottle holds 3.79 liters. How much is this in kiloliters?

_____ kiloliter

6. Pedro divides 0.5 liters of bleach evenly into 10-milliliter graduated cylinders. How many cylinders does he use?

_____ graduated cylinders

Lesson 5.1 Units of Length (millimeters, centimeters, decimeters, meters, and kilometers)

Read the problem carefully and solve. Show your work under each question.

Students from Washington Middle School participate in the regional track and field competition. Featured events include distance running, relay races, standing long jump, and the discus throw.

Helpful Hint

Millimeters (mm), **centimeters** (cm), **decimeters** (dm), **meters** (m), and **kilometers** (km) are metric measures of length.

10 mm = 1 cm	1 mm = 0.1 cm
1,000 mm = 1 m	1 mm = 0.001 m
100 cm = 1 m	1 cm = 0.01 m
1,000 m = 1 km	1 m = 0.001 km
1m = 10 dm	

1. A half-marathon is 21.0975 kilometers. How many meters is this?

_____ meters

2. Armando won the standing long jump competition. He jumped 2.43 meters. How many centimeters did Armando jump?

_____ centimeters

3. The diameter of a discus is 220 millimeters. How many decimeters is this?

_____ decimeters

4. During a 4 × 400-meter relay race, how many kilometers does a team run?

_____ kilometers

5. If the length of the track is 400 meters, how many times must a student run around the track during a 5-kilometer race?

_____ times

Lesson 5.2 Liquid Volume (milliliters, liters, and kiloliters)

Read the problem carefully and solve. Show your work under each question.

Mr. Espinoza is teaching about energy conservation. He asks his students to record the amount of time and how their families use water during the course of a week. Their records should include the time spent taking showers or baths and brushing their teeth. They should also include the time they water the lawn or if they wash the family car.

Helpful Hint

Milliliters (mL), **liters** (L), and **kiloliters** (kL) are metric measures of liquid volume.

1 L = 1,000 mL

1 kL = 1,000 L

1 mL = 0.001 L

1 L = 0.001 kL

1. Felicia's bathtub can hold 37.84 liters of water when a person is taking a bath. How many kiloliters of water is this?

_____ kiloliter

2. If a 5-minute shower uses 9,460 milliliters of water, how many liters will Noah use each time he takes a shower?

_____ liters

3. Maurice fills a bucket with 2.84 liters of water to wash the family car. How many milliliters of water will he use?

_____ milliliters

4. If a sprinkler system uses 0.1324 kiloliters of water each hour, how many liters of water are used in three hours?

_____ liters

5. A family of 5 brushes their teeth twice a day. If each person uses 236.5 milliliters each time they brush their teeth, how many liters of water would this family use?

_____ liters

Lesson 5.3 Weight (milligrams, grams, kilograms, and metric tons)

Read the problem carefully and solve. Show your work under each question.

Zoe made trail mix for her friends and family. The trail mix has oat cereal, granola, raisins, dried fruit, pecans, walnuts, pine nuts, and sunflower seeds.

Helpful Hint

Milligrams (mg), **grams** (g), and **kilograms** (kg) are metric measures of weight.

1 g = 1,000 mg   1 mg = 0.001 g

1 kg = 1,000 g   1 metric ton = 1,000 kg

1. A box of oat cereal contains 425,000 milligrams of cereal. How many grams of cereal does the box contain?

_____ grams

2. A bag contains 255 grams of raisins. How many milligrams of raisins is this?

_____ milligrams

3. Zoe combines 227 grams of pecans, 198 grams of walnuts, and 17 grams of pine nuts for the trail mix. How many kilograms of nuts are in the mixture?

_____ kilogram

4. One batch of trail mix weighs 1.6 kilograms. How many batches of trail mix could be made from one metric ton of trail mix?

_____ batches

5. Zoe fills 25 bags with a total of 1.6 kilograms of trail mix. How many grams of trail mix is in each bag?

_____ grams

Check What You Learned

Metric Measurement

Read the problem carefully and solve. Show your work under each question.

Students from the Johnson Middle School participate in the regional swim meet. Featured swimming events include freestyle, backstroke, butterfly, and relay races. Students will also compete in several diving events.

1. The diving board at the competition is 10 meters long. How long is this in centimeters?

_____ centimeters

4. Heath weighs 56,090 grams. What is the difference in kilograms of his weight and the weight limit of 113.4 kilograms for the diving board?

_____ kilograms

2. The swimming pool is 0.05 kilometers long. Vanessa participates in the 200-meter freestyle event. How many laps of the pool does she swim?

_____ laps

5. The swimming pool is filled with 2,500 kiloliters of water. How many liters of water is that?

_____ liters

3. The diving board has a weight limit of 113.4 kilograms. How many grams is that?

_____ grams

6. Five liters of chlorine and 250 centiliters of a cleaning agent are added to the pool. How many total milliliters of liquid are added to the pool?

_____ milliliters

Mid-Test Chapters 1–5

Read the problem carefully and solve. Show your work under each question.

A local bookstore has a variety of fiction books in its inventory. The store has 3,218 mystery novels, 6,728 thrillers, 313 westerns, 10,454 romance novels, and 855 crime books.

---

1. How many fiction books are in the store?

_____ books

2. How many more romance books are there than thrillers?

_____ more books

3. Carmon bought 2 thrillers at $7.99 each, 3 romance novels at $9.99 each, and a western for $25.95. How much did Carmon spend?

_____

4. Mandy bought 4 mystery novels and spent $43.83. If she paid $2.63 in taxes, and each book cost the same amount, how much did each book cost?

_____

5. The owner of the bookstore wants to feature the crime books. He displays $\frac{2}{5}$ of his inventory at the front of the store. How many books does he display?

_____ books

6. The westerns in the store's inventory were written by 4 different authors. Author A wrote $\frac{1}{4}$ of the books, author B wrote $\frac{5}{16}$ of the books, and author C wrote $\frac{3}{8}$ of the books. What part of the inventory of westerns did author D write?

_____ of the books

Mid-Test Chapters 1–5

Read the problem carefully and solve. Show your work under each question.

The students in Mrs. Yi's art class are painting ceramic pieces and making sculptures. The students will display their work at the school's annual art exhibit.

1. Craig is making a model of a building that is 125 feet tall. His model is 5 feet tall and 9 feet wide. How wide is the actual building?

   _____ feet

4. Three 10-piece acrylic paint sets sell for $39.99. Mrs. Yi needs 125 sets for her classes. How much does Mrs. Yi spend on acrylic paint?

   _____

2. Jordan can paint 3 small ceramic pieces in 45 minutes. At that rate, how long will it take her to paint 10 pieces?

   _____ minutes

5. Sculpting clay costs $10.75 for 14 ounces. Mason needs 126 ounces for his model. How much does Mason spend on clay?

   _____

6. It takes 75 minutes to bake 15 ceramic pieces in a kiln. How long will it take to bake 3 pieces?

   _____ minutes

3. Norris is making a model of a truck. The actual truck is 192 inches long and has a height of 72 inches. If the model is 6 inches high, how long is the model?

   _____ inches

Mid-Test Chapters 1–5

Read the problem carefully and solve. Show your work under each question.

Andre is moving into a new house. He needs to purchase a new refrigerator, stove, microwave oven, and dishwasher. He shops at Discount Appliance during their special sale event.

1. Discount Appliance is offering 15% off the entire purchase of two or more items. Write this number as a decimal and fraction in simplest form.

   _____ and _____

2. The stove Andre likes costs $1,019. Discount Appliance is offering this stove at 10% off. How much will Andre pay for the stove?

   _____

3. A refrigerator normally costs $789.75. It is on sale for $663.39. What is the percent of the discount?

   _____

4. Andre saves $49.98 on a countertop microwave oven. The microwave oven was discounted 25%. What was the original cost of the microwave oven?

   _____

5. The salesman at Discount Appliance offers Andre financing for his purchase. Andre can get a loan at simple interest of 3.5%. If Andre's purchase totals $3,238, how much interest does he pay after 3 years?

   _____

6. Andre places $1,000 in a savings account that yields 2% compounded semi-annually. How much does Andre have in the account after 2 years? Round to the nearest cent.

   _____

Mid-Test Chapters 1–5

Read the problem carefully and solve. Show your work under each question.

Trey is interested in aviation. He wants to learn everything he can about his favorite airplane. He does research and writes a report for his language class.

1. Trey learns that the capacity of the airplane is 81,600 kilograms. How many grams is this?

_____ grams

2. The airplane's tail height is 63 feet 5 inches. How many inches is this?

_____ inches

3. The airplane usually cruises at 36,000 feet. How many yards is this?

_____ yards

4. On average, the airplane can travel 9,260,000 meters without refueling. How many kilometers is this?

_____ kilometers

5. Trey finds that a new version of the airplane has been made. The wingspan has been lengthened from 195 feet 8 inches to 211 feet 5 inches. What is the difference in the wingspans?

_____ feet _____ inches

6. Trey finds that the fuel capacity is increased by 3,965 gallons 3 quarts. The original fuel capacity is 48,445 gallons 2 quarts. What is the fuel capacity of the new version of the airplane?

_____ gallons _____ quart

Check What You Know

Probability and Statistics

Answer the questions by interpreting data from each graph.

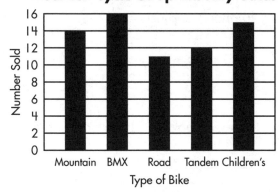

Corner Cycle Shop Weekly Sales

Number Sold (y-axis: 0, 2, 4, 6, 8, 10, 12, 14, 16)

Type of Bike (x-axis: Mountain, BMX, Road, Tandem, Children's)

1. What type of bike did the Corner Cycle Shop sell the most of?

_____

2. How many more children's bikes were sold than road bikes?

_____

3. What is the median of this data?

_____

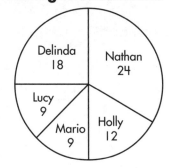

Books Read by Students During First Semester

Delinda 18 · Nathan 24 · Lucy 9 · Mario 9 · Holly 12

4. How many books were read by the students?

_____ books

5. How many degrees of the circle are used to represent the number of books read by Nathan?

_____

6. Delinda represents what percentage of the total number of books read?

_____

How many degrees of the circle are used to represent this percentage?

_____

Raffle Tickets Sold

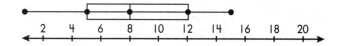

(number line: 2, 4, 6, 8, 10, 12, 14, 16, 18, 20)

7. What is the interquartile range of the raffle tickets sold?

_____

8. What is the median of the data?

_____

9. What value is at the upper extreme of the data?

_____

NAME _____

Check What You Know

Probability and Statistics

Chandra made a list of the daily high temperatures for West City during the first 15 days of April. Her list is as follows: 55°, 62°, 65°, 53°, 55°, 60°, 65°, 63°, 53°, 72°, 64°, 63°, 68°, 70°, 65°.

1. What is the median temperature?

_____

2. What is the mode of the data?

_____

3. What is the mean temperature?

_____

4. What is the range in temperatures?

_____

Use the spinner to determine the probability of the following events. Write your answer as a fraction in simplest form.

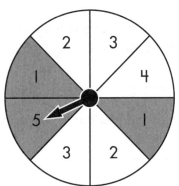

5. spinner stopping on a gray section

_____

6. spinner stopping on a 2

_____

7. spinner stopping on an odd number

_____

8. Sean has 4 college jerseys with logos of an eagle, a bear, a dog and a mule. His 3 hats have logos of an oriole, blue jay and cardinal. How many different combinations of jerseys and hats can he make? Make a tree diagram to solve.

Lesson 6.1 Bar Graphs

Read the problem carefully and solve. Show your work under each question.

Ethan surveyed his classmates about their favorite types of movies. He made the bar graph to the right to show the results.

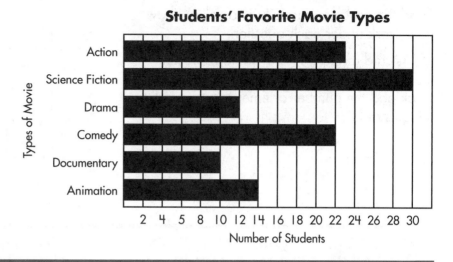

Students' Favorite Movie Types

Helpful Hint

Bar graphs are used to compare data. The bars compare data in different categories.

1. How many students did Ethan survey?

_____ students

2. Which type of movies do most of the students say is their favorite?

_____

3. How many more students prefer science fiction than drama?

_____ students

4. How many students named action movies as their favorite type?

_____ students

5. How many fewer students prefer comedy than action movies?

_____ students

Lesson 6.2 Histograms

Read the problem carefully and solve. Show your work under each question.

Mr. Quaid made a histogram to represent the number of hours that students study per week and the number of times they passed his quizzes.

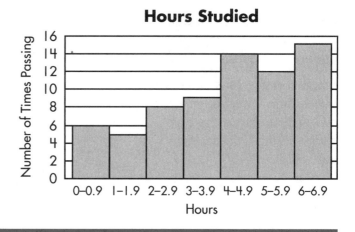

Hours Studied

Helpful Hint

A **histogram** compares categories that are represented as intervals of the same size. The height of the bars represents the number of times something occurs. Because the data represent continuous values, the bars touch each other.

1. What does each bar represent?

_____

2. How many quizzes did students pass if they studied 0–0.9 hours?

_____quizzes

3. If a student studied between 4 and 4.9 hours, how many quizzes did she pass?

_____ quizzes

4. Which interval of hours studied resulted in the greatest number of passed quizzes?

_____hours

5. Based on the histogram, if a student studies 3–3.9 hours per week, how many quizzes will he pass?

_____ quizzes

Lesson 6.3 Line Graphs

Read the problem carefully and solve.
Show your work under each question.

Mrs. Dolby likes to keep track of the number of students who stay after school for her extra help sessions. She makes a line graph to record this information.

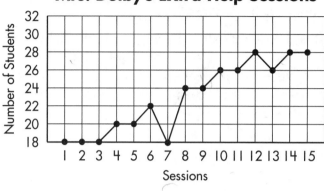

Mrs. Dolby's Extra Help Sessions

Helpful Hint

A **line graph** shows how data changes over time.

1. How many students attended the tenth extra help session?

    _____ students

2. How many extra help sessions did Mrs. Dolby hold?

    _____ extra help sessions

3. What is the greatest number of students that attended an individual session?

    _____ students

4. How many more students attended session 10 than session 6?

    _____ more students

5. What was the total attendance number for sessions 3, 5, 7, and 11 combined?

    _____ students

Lesson 6.4 Circle Graphs

Read the problem carefully and solve. Show your work under each question.

It is a requirement at Pine Hills Middle School that all eighth-grade students participate in one of the music groups. The circle graph on the right shows the percent of students enrolled in each activity. There are a total of 420 eighth-grade students.

Students in the Music Program

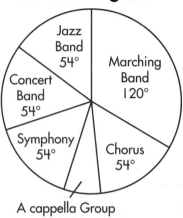

> **Helpful Hint**
>
> A **circle graph** shows the relationship between parts of a group. The circle represents the whole group, and the sections represent the parts of the group.

1. How many degrees of the circle are used to represent the a cappella group?

_____ degrees

2. What fraction of the students participates in the marching band? What percent is this?

_____ of the students

_____

3. What percent of the students are in the chorus?

_____

4. How many students are in the concert band?

_____ students

5. How many students are members of the jazz band and symphony combined?

_____ students

Lesson 6.5 Scattergrams

Read the problem carefully and solve.
Show your work under each question.

Mr. Hernandez asked his students to
conduct a survey for their statistics unit.
Byron decided to ask people between the
ages of 5 and 20 what their shoe size
was. The scattergram at the right shows the
results of his survey.

Age and Shoe Size Poll Results

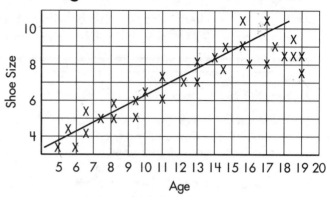

Helpful Hint

A **scattergram** is a graph that shows the
relationship between two sets of data. To
help see the relationship clearly, a **line of
best fit** can be drawn. The line is drawn so
that there are about the same number of
data points above and below the line.

1. Which two pieces of data are being
compared by this scattergram?

_____

2. Is the correlation positive or negative?

_____

3. How many people were surveyed?

_____

4. Where are there outliers for this
scattergram?

_____

5. What is a possible explanation?

_____

_____

_____

Lesson 6.6 Measures of Central Tendency

Read the problem carefully and solve. Show your work under each question.

Each year, Jeffrey keeps track of his bowling tournament scores and records the data. His results for this year are: 221, 186, 171, 126, 208, and 186.

Helpful Hint

The **mean** is the average of a set of numbers. The **median** is the middle number of a set of numbers. If there are two middle numbers, the median is the average of the two. The **mode** is the number that appears most often in a set of numbers. The **range** is the difference between the greatest and least numbers in the set.

1. What is the mean of Jeffrey's scores?

   _____

2. What is the median of Jeffrey's scores?

   _____

3. What are the mode and range of Jeffrey's scores?

   mode _____

   range _____

4. How would the median change if Jeffrey bowled one more game and scored 171?

   _____

5. Last year, Jeffrey's scores were: 161, 200, 142, 202, 201 and 156. Which measure of central tendency changed the most from last year, and by how much?

   _____

   _____

   _____

Lesson 6.7 Frequency Tables

Complete the chart with fractions in simplest form. Then, answer the questions.

For Mr. Hernandez' statistics unit, Amira decided to ask some seventh graders how many hats they had. She made a frequency table to show the results of his survey.

> **Helpful Hint**
>
> A **frequency table** lists the range of scores, the number in each range, the cumulative frequency, and the relative frequency. The relative frequency compares the number in each range with the total.

Number of Hats

	Range	Number in Range	Cumulative Frequency	Relative Frequency
1.	(0–2)	12	12	
2.	(3–5)	10	22	
3.	(6–8)	6	28	
4.	(9–11)	2	30	

5. How many seventh graders were polled?

   _____ seventh graders

6. How many students had between 0 and 5 hats?

   _____

Lesson 6.8 Line Plots

Read the problem carefully and solve. Show your work under each question.

Ella works at Salad Bar King where they offer 18 different items in the premier salad bar. For ordering purposes, the manager asks Ella to keep track of how many items each customer takes. She records the results on a line plot.

> **Helpful Hint**
>
> A **line plot** uses a number line to clearly illustrate the frequency of data. Each piece of data is represented by an "X."

Interpret the line plot to answer the questions that follow.

Number of Items Taken in a Salad Bar

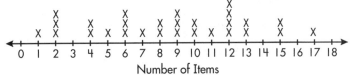

Number of Items

1. How many data points are there? What is the mode of the data?

   _____ _____

2. What is the median of the data?

   _____

3. What is the mean of the data? Round to the nearest tenth.

   _____

4. How many people chose 10 or more items?

   _____

5. What is the range?

   _____

Lesson 6.9 Box-and-Whisker Plots

Read the problem carefully and solve. Show your work under each question.

Sixth-grade students at Western Middle School are collecting new and used books to donate to the community center. Yuri is responsible for recording the number of books the students in each homeroom contribute. The box-and-whisker plot below shows the results.

Book Contributions

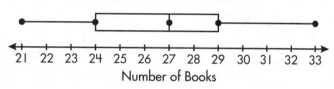

Number of Books

Helpful Hint

A **box-and-whisker plot** makes it easy to see the median and quartiles of a data set.

1. What is the median number of books the students contribute?

_____

2. What is the range of the number of books collected?

_____

3. What is the interquartile range in this data?

_____

4. What is the lower extreme of the data on this box-and-whisker plot?

_____

5. Between which two numbers of books are the top 25% of the homerooms?

_____

Lesson 6.10 Tree Diagrams

Read the problem carefully and solve. Show your work under each question.

On Saturdays, Veronica takes care of her 5-year-old neighbor, Bailey. She is responsible for helping Bailey get dressed, preparing her lunch, and planning activities.

> **Helpful Hint**
>
> **Sample space** means all possible outcomes of an experiment.
>
> A **tree diagram** is useful to find the number of possible combinations.

1. Bailey has 2 favorite pairs of sneakers, a white pair and a blue pair. She has to choose from 3 different shirts; green, yellow, or pink. She has 2 pairs of pants, black and tan. How many different combinations could Bailey choose? Make a tree diagram to solve.

2. Bailey is painting a vase or a cup one color. Her choices of colors are red, blue, or green. How many different combinations can she choose from? Make a tree diagram to solve.

3. Veronica offers to make Bailey a sandwich for lunch. Her choices are ham or turkey on white, rye, or wheat bread. How many different combinations of meat and bread does Bailey have to choose from? Make a tree diagram to solve.

4. Bailey needs to decide which "friend" to bring to the annual Bear Tea Party. She has a teddy bear and a panda bear. Since it is cool out, Bailey needs to wear a jacket. Bailey has a red or green jacket. How many different combinations of jackets and bears does Bailey have to choose from? Make a tree diagram to solve.

5. Veronica offers Bailey a yogurt snack when they return from the library. Bailey can choose vanilla, strawberry, blueberry, or banana yogurt. The stir-in choices are granola, raisins, or walnuts. How many different combinations of yogurt and stir-ins can Bailey choose from? Make a tree diagram to solve.

Lesson 6.11 Matrices

Read the problem carefully and solve. Show your work under each question.

Pilar polled third, fourth, and fifth graders to find out what their favorite subject is: math, science, reading, history, or geography. The matrix on the right shows the data she collected.

	M	S	R	H	G
3rd	[9	9	13	3	12]
4th	[8	15	17	6	15]
5th	[12	5	20	2	16]

> **Helpful Hint**
>
> A **matrix** is a special way of organizing data visually. It is an arrangement of rows and columns. Each row is in brackets.

1. What size matrix did Pilar make?

_____

2. Which subject is the least favorite for all three grade levels?

_____

3. Which subject do the students at all levels prefer?

_____

4. Which two subjects are liked equally with polled fourth graders?

_____

5. Which two subjects are liked equally with polled third graders?

_____

Lesson 6.12 Calculating Probability

Read the problem carefully and solve. Show your work under each question.

Umberto contributes a bag of colored balloons as part of the decorations for the class party. The bag contains 3 red balloons, 2 blue balloons, 1 purple balloon, 4 yellow balloons, and 6 green balloons. His friends will help him blow up the balloons.

Helpful Hint

Probability can be shown as a fraction in simplest form.

1. Austin reaches in the bag. What is the probability that Austin will choose a red balloon?

   _____

2. Grace picks a balloon. What is the probability that she chooses a yellow balloon?

   _____

3. Umberto chooses his balloon. What is the probability that he will pick a blue or a green balloon?

   _____

4. What is the probability that Virginia will pick a red or yellow balloon?

   _____

5. What is the probability that Justin will choose a red, blue, or green balloon?

   _____

Check What You Learned

Probability and Statistics

Answer the questions by interpreting data from each graph.

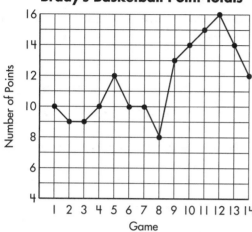

Brady's Basketball Point Totals

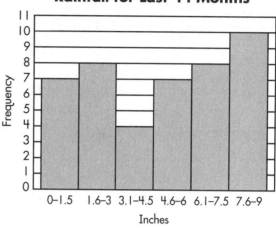

Rainfall for Last 44 Months

1. For how many games did Brady track his total points?

   _____ games

2. How many points did Brady score during game 9?

   _____ points

3. How many points did Brady score during games 3, 4, 5, and 6 combined?

   _____ points

4. What is the difference between the number of points Brady scored in week 12 and week 9?

   _____ points

5. What is the interval represented by each bar?

   _____

6. How many months did it rain between 0 and 1.5 inches?

   _____

7. How many months did it rain between 7.6 and 9 inches?

   _____ inches

8. How many months did it rain less than 3 inches?

   _____

CHAPTER 6 POSTTEST

Check What You Learned

Probability and Statistics

Trivia Game Scores

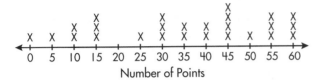

Number of Points

1. How many data points are there?

   _____

2. What is the median of the scores?

   _____

3. What is the mean score?

   _____

Ian made this matrix. It shows the results of his survey of left-handed and right-handed students and whether they liked corn, peas, or green beans. Students could choose more than one vegetable.

$$\begin{array}{lccc} & C & P & G \\ \text{Left-handed} & [28 & 34 & 18] \\ \text{Right-handed} & [31 & 6 & 42] \end{array}$$

4. Which vegetable is the least favorite of left-handed students?

   _____

5. Which vegetable is the least favorite of right-handed students?

   _____

6. Can you tell from the matrix how many students were included in Ian's poll?

   _____

Fill in the missing data in the frequency table. Then, answer the questions.

Scores on a Fitness Exam

	Range	Frequency	Cumulative Frequency	Relative Frequency
7.	(50–59)	2	2	
8.	(60–69)	2	4	
9.	(70–79)	4	8	
10.	(80–89)	8	16	
11.	(90–99)	4	20	

12. How many students' scores are there in the table? _____

NAME _____

 Check What You Know

Geometry

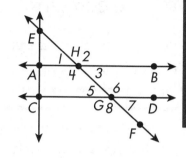

Read the problem carefully and solve. Show your work under each question.

Connor is planning a scenic trip for his family and is using a map. He places capital letters on the map to signify towns he wants to visit. He notices that the map for his trip contains some figures he recently learned about. Connor uses numbers to name the angles that are formed. The figure on the right shows the map of Old Port County.

---

1. The roads represented by $\overleftrightarrow{AB}$ and $\overleftrightarrow{CD}$ are the same distance apart at all points. What term describes this relationship?

_____

2. Connor writes $\overline{HG}$ to represent the distance from Hillsboro (*H*) to Gardner (*G*) using a symbol and letters. What does $\overline{HG}$ mean?

_____

3. Ellisville (*E*), Hillsboro (*H*), and Adams (*A*) form $\angle EHA$. What are the three parts of $\angle EHA$?

_____ _____ _____

4. Which two lines form transversals? Use a symbol and letters to write your answer.

_____

5. Which of the numbered angles are obtuse?

_____

6. Which pairs of numbered angles are vertical angles?

_____

7. Which pairs of numbered angles are alternate interior angles?

_____

8. The towns of Ellisville (*E*), Copper Cove (*C*), and Gainesville (*G*) form a triangle. Name this triangle based on its angles.

_____

CHAPTER 7 PRETEST

Spectrum Enrichment Math
Grade 8

Check What You Know
Chapter 7
59

NAME _____

Check What You Know

Geometry

Read the problem carefully and solve. Show your work under each question.

Connor is looking at other destinations for his trip. He uses a map to help determine the relative locations of some towns.

1. Connor's possible plan for two days of his trip is shown below. For the fist day, Connor draws the route traveling east from Freetown (F) to Victory (V) and then south to Watertown (W). What type of triangle does this form?

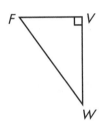

_____

2. For the second day, the route goes west from Freetown (F) to Middleboro (M) and then south, to Yarmouth (Y). Name the angle formed by the route using symbols.

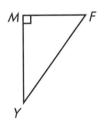

_____

3. The routes of Connor's previous trips form 2 triangles. What is the transformation of the first triangle to the second triangle?

_____

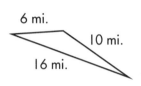 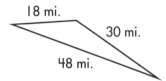

4. The distance from Freetown (F) to Victory (V) is 30 miles and the distance from Freetown (F) to Watertown (W) is 50 miles. What is the distance from Victory to Watertown?

_____ miles

5. Two lakes on the state map are similar triangles. The boundaries of the smaller lake are 6, 10, and 16 miles. How long is the third boundary of the larger lake if the smallest boundary is 18 miles and the longest boundary is 48 miles?

_____ miles

Lesson 7.1 Points and Lines

Read the problem carefully and solve. Show your work under each question.

Garrick is interested in studying astronomy. He is looking at a map of various constellations and star formations. He labels four of the stars *S, T, A, R* and uses a ruler to make straight lines to connect some of them.

Helpful Hint

A **point** is named by a capital letter.

A **line** is named by choosing any two points on it. $\overleftrightarrow{AB}$ can also be written as $\overleftrightarrow{BA}$.

A **line segment** is named by its two endpoints. $\overline{DE}$ can also be written as $\overline{ED}$.

1. The drawing below identifies the location of star *T*. Name the figure.

_____

2. Garrick draws a line connecting points *S* and *R*. Name the figure using letters. If you can, name the figure in more than one way.

_____

3. Garrick draws a line through points *A* and *S*. Name the figure using letters. If you can, name the figure in more than one way.

$$\xleftrightarrow{\quad \underset{A}{\bullet} \qquad \underset{S}{\bullet} \quad}$$

_____

4. He draws $\overline{RA}$ next. What does this symbol represent? Draw it.

_____

5. Finally, Garrick draws $\overleftrightarrow{TR}$. What does this symbol represent? Draw it.

_____

Lesson 7.2 Rays and Angles

Read the problem carefully and solve. Show your work under each question.

Leslie spends three afternoons a week at the archery range. She participates in competitions once a month. She takes notes each time she practices so that she can study to improve her performance.

> **Helpful Hint**
>
> A **ray** is always named starting with its endpoint. $\overrightarrow{CD}$ can not be written as $\overrightarrow{DC}$.
>
> An **angle** is formed from two rays with a common endpoint, called the **vertex**.

1. Leslie draws the figure below to show that she pointed her arrow up. Name the figure using letters. Name the figure in more than one way if you can.

_____

2. Leslie draws the figure below to show the angle of her first shot. Name the figure using letters. Name the figure in more than one way if you can.

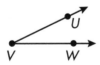

_____

3. Leslie draws $\overrightarrow{PQ}$. What does this symbol represent? Draw the figure.

_____

4. The figure below shows two more of Leslie's shots. Name the figure in more than one way if you can.

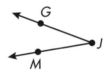

_____

5. Leslie draws $\angle PTR$. What does this symbol represent? Draw the figure.

_____

Lesson 7.3 Measuring Angles

Read the problem carefully and solve. Show your work under each question.

Quinn is a physical therapist that helps patients after their surgery or with other physical ailments. One of his jobs includes keeping track of the progress his patients make. He will often measure how far a patient can move his or her arms or legs and then record the progress on a chart.

Helpful Hint

An **acute** angle measures less than 90°.

A **right** angle measures exactly 90°.

An **obtuse** angle measures more than 90° and less than 180°.

1. The figure below is a record of how far Bradley can move his knee after surgery. Write whether the angle is obtuse, acute, or right. Then, measure the angle.

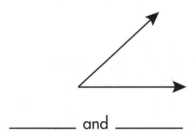

_____ and _____

2. Paige fell and broke her arm. The figure below shows how far she can move her arm. Write whether the angle is obtuse, acute, or right. Then, measure the angle.

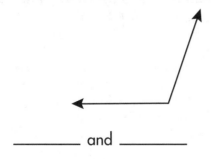

_____ and _____

3. Quinn expects all his patients' legs to form the angle below when seated. Write whether the angle is obtuse, acute, or right. Then, measure the angle.

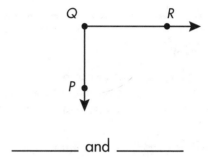

_____ and _____

4. After a knee injury, Gavin could bend his knee as far as the figure below. Write whether the angle is obtuse, acute, or right. Then, measure the angle.

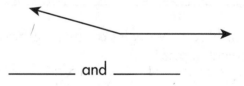

_____ and _____

5. Quinn gives his patients a number of exercises to do each day as part of their therapy. The figure below shows the angle of one of the leg exercises. Write whether the angle is obtuse, acute, or right. Then, measure the angle.

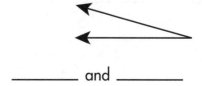

_____ and _____

Lesson 7.4 Vertical, Supplementary, and Complementary Angles

Read the problem carefully and solve. Show your work under each question.

Wyatt makes a map of the campground he will visit with his family. He uses angles and intersecting lines to represent the streets and paths. He decides to label the lines and angles on his map and plans to measure some of the angles.

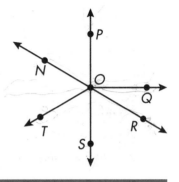

Helpful Hint

Vertical angles are formed when two straight lines intersect. They are opposite angles and are equal. Vertical angles are **congruent**.

Two angles are **supplementary** if their sum is 180°.

Two angles are **complementary** if their sum is 90°.

An **angle bisector** is a line drawn through the vertex of an angle that divides it into two angles that have the same measure.

1. Which pairs of angles on the map are vertical angles?

   ∠SOP and ∠RON

2. Are ∠NOP and ∠POR complementary, supplementary, or vertical?

   supplementary

3. Are ∠QOR and ∠SOR supplementary, complementary, or vertical?

   complementary

4. If $\overrightarrow{OT}$ is an angle bisector, and ∠SOT = 60°, what is the measure of ∠NOT?

   60

5. If the measure of ∠QOR is 30°, what is the measure of ∠NOQ?

   150

Lesson 7.5 Transversals

Read the problem carefully and solve. Show your work under each question.

The sketch at the right is a drawing of the streets in Becca's neighborhood. She labels the streets by their names. She labels the angles the streets form with the numbers 1 to 8.

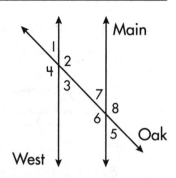

Helpful Hint

Parallel lines are two lines that will never meet.

A **transversal** is a line that intersects 2 parallel lines.

Adjacent angles are any 2 angles that are next to one another.

Alternate interior angles are those that are inside the parallel lines and opposite one another.

Alternate exterior angles are those that are outside the parallel lines and opposite one another.

3. Which pairs of angles are adjacent angles?

∠12 ∠14 ∠32
~~∠24~~ ∠34 ∠78 ∠76
∠85 ∠65

4. Which angles are alternate interior angles?

∠26 ∠37

5. Which angles are alternate exterior angles?

∠18 ∠45

1. Which two streets are parallel?

Main and west

2. Which street is the transversal?

Oak

Lesson 7.6 Classifying Triangles (by angles)

Read the problem carefully and solve. Show your work under each question.

Sierra makes stained glass sun-catchers for her aunt's crafts store. This week, she will focus on making sun-catchers out of three different types of triangles. She will focus on triangles with different sizes of angles. She will use a protractor to measure the angles.

> **Helpful Hint**
>
> **Acute triangles** have three angles that measure less than 90°.
>
> **Right triangles** have one right angle. Right angles measure 90°.
>
> **Obtuse triangles** have one angle that measures greater than 90°.

1. Sierra's first sun-catcher is shaped like the triangle below. Identify this triangle as acute, right, or obtuse.

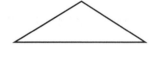

_____

2. The sun-catcher that people buy the most is shaped like the triangle below. Identify this triangle as acute, right, or obtuse.

_____

3. Sierra's favorite sun-catcher is shaped like the triangle below. Identify this triangle as acute, right, or obtuse.

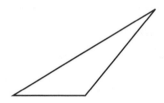

_____

4. Aunt Ursula's favorite sun-catcher is shaped like the triangle below. Identify this triangle as acute, right, or obtuse.

_____

5. The least popular sun-catcher is shaped like the triangle below. Identify this triangle as acute, right, or obtuse.

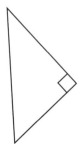

_____

Lesson 7.7 Classifying Triangles (by sides)

Read the problem carefully and solve. Show your work under each question.

Sierra's sun-catchers are so popular that Aunt Ursula asks her to make some new designs. Sierra decides that she will focus on the side lengths of the triangles. She will use a ruler to measure the sides.

> **Helpful Hint**
>
> An **equilateral** triangle has 3 sides of the same length.
>
> An **isosceles** triangle has at least 2 sides of the same length.
>
> A **scalene** triangle has no sides of the same length.

1. Sierra's first design is shaped like the triangle below. Identify this triangle as equilateral, isosceles, or scalene.

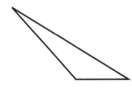

_____

2. Aunt Ursula's suggestion for a new design is a triangle shaped like the one below. Identify this triangle as equilateral, isosceles, or scalene.

_____

3. The most popular sun-catcher among children is shaped like the triangle below. Identify this triangle as equilateral, isosceles, or scalene.

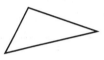

_____

4. Sierra's new favorite design is shaped like the triangle below. Identify this triangle as equilateral, isosceles, or scalene.

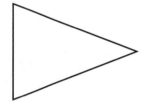

_____

5. Aunt Ursula plans on having a sale on the sun-catchers shaped like the triangle below. Identify this triangle as equilateral, isosceles, or scalene.

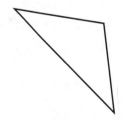

_____

Lesson 7.8 Similar Triangles

Read the problem carefully and solve. Show your work under each question.

The Kite Club is the newest after-school club at Kennedy Middle School. Mr. Underwood asks the student members to make a drawing of the type of kite they would like to build. He tells them that their sketches should be drawn to scale.

Helpful Hint

Two triangles are **similar** if their corresponding angles are congruent and the lengths of their corresponding sides are proportional.

1. Zach wants to make a kite that has a 14-inch base and sides of 21 inches. His sketch has sides of 12 inches. To make the triangles similar, how many inches should the base of his triangle be?

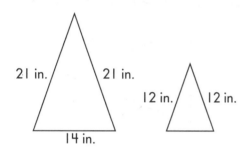

_____ inches

2. Nadia's sketch shows a triangle with sides of 10 inches, 16 inches, and 17 inches. One of the sides of her actual kite will be 30 inches and another side will be 48 inches. What is the length of the third side?

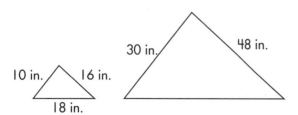

_____ inches

3. Crystal wants her kite to have a height of 48 inches, a base of 36 inches, and a diagonal length of 60 inches. Her sketch shows the height as 8 inches and the base as 6 inches. How long is the diagonal of the triangle in the sketch?

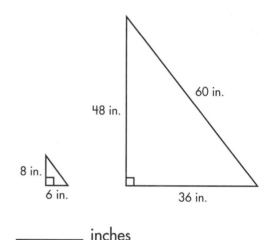

_____ inches

4. Luke's kite has side lengths of 36 inches, 60 inches, and 96 inches. The shortest side of his sketch is 3 inches, and the longest side is 8 inches. How long is the third side?

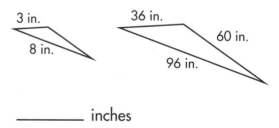

_____ inches

Lesson 7.9 Squares and Square Roots

Read the problem carefully and solve. Show your work under each question.

Student members of the Environmental Club at Armstrong Intermediate School volunteer to help the members of the city's garden club plant flowers and bulbs in the town square. Each student is given a number of plants or bulbs and assigned a square area to plant their flowers.

Helpful Hint

The **square** of a number is that number times itself.

$7^2 = 7 \times 7 = 49$

The **square root** of a number is the number that when multiplied by itself, equals that number.

$\sqrt{49} = 7$

1. Brianna has 25 geranium plants. She finds $\sqrt{25}$ to determine how many rows she will plant. How many rows of geraniums will Brianna plant?

    _____ rows

2. Mrs. Friedman gives Spencer 49 tulip bulbs to plant. Spencer finds $\sqrt{49}$ to determine how many rows he will plant. How many rows of tulip bulbs will he plant?

    _____ rows

3. Marigolds are Roxanne's favorite flower. She has 144 marigold plants. She finds $\sqrt{144}$ to determine how many rows she will plant. How many rows of marigolds will Roxanne plant?

    _____ rows

4. Monique offers to plant the daffodil bulbs. She is given 121 bulbs. Monique finds $\sqrt{121}$ to determine how many rows she will plant. How many rows of daffodils will Monique plant?

    _____ rows

5. Parker is given 67 petunia plants. He estimates $\sqrt{67}$ to figure out the number of rows he will be able to fill in his square area. Which two square roots is $\sqrt{67}$ between? Which number is it closest to?

    _____ _____ _____

Lesson 7.10 Using the Pythagorean Theorem

Read the problem carefully and solve. Show your work under each question.

Morgan is shopping for a new computer and a new television. He takes a trip to the local electronics store to gather information about sizes and costs.

Helpful Hint

The **Pythagorean Theorem** states that the sum of the squares of the sides of a right triangle is equal to the sum of the square of the hypotenuse.

$a^2 + b^2 = c^2$

---

1. Laptop computer A has a screen with a width of 12 inches and a height of 9 inches. How long is the diagonal of the computer screen?

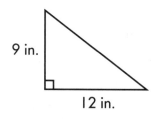

_____ inches

2. The screen of television A has a diagonal of 50 inches. Its height is 30 inches. What is the width of the television screen?

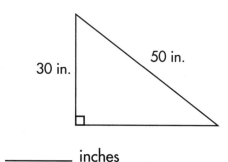

_____ inches

3. The diagonal of the screen of laptop computer B is 17 inches. The width of the screen is 15 inches. What is the height of the computer screen?

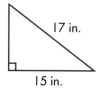

_____ inches

4. Morgan really likes television B. The screen has a width of 30 inches and a height of 21 inches. About how long is the diagonal of the screen?

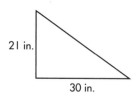

about _____ inches

5. The sales person shows Morgan desktop computer C. The height of the screen is 13 inches and the width is 20 inches. About how long is the diagonal of the screen?

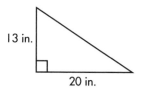

about _____ inches

Lesson 7.11 The Pythagorean Theorem and Similar Right Triangles

Read the problem carefully and solve. Show your work under each question.

Tripp is attending a camp for the summer. He will help assemble structures and plan events.

1. Tripp helps set up a new tent next to an old tent. The rope from the tent poles to the stakes forms similar triangles as shown. How tall is the pole of the new tent?

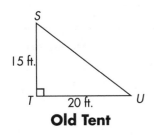
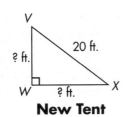

Old Tent   **New Tent**

_____ feet

2. The American flag and the scout flag cast shadows as shown in the figure below. How tall are the poles?

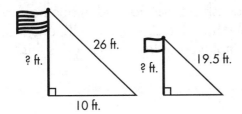

The American flagpole is _____ feet tall.

The scout flagpole is _____ feet tall.

3. The poles and rope for two sleeping tents form similar triangles as depicted in the figures below. What is the height of the pole of the larger tent?

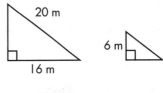

_____ meters

4. Two guy wires steady the camp's radio antenna as shown. How far from the ground is guy wire 1 attached?

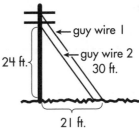

_____ feet

5. The course for the swimming test is shown below. Advanced swimmers begin at point S, swim to point T, proceed to point A, and return to point S. How many meters do advanced swimmers swim?

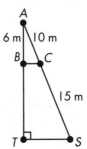

_____ meters

Lesson 7.12 Transformations

Read the problem carefully and solve. Show your work under each question.

Students in the math club are playing a game during their afternoon meeting. The object of the game is to move objects so that the given image is either translated, rotated, reflected, or dilated. The graph on the right shows Hunter's graph once all his moves are made.

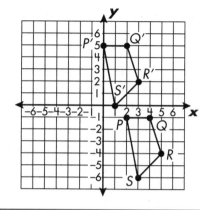

Helpful Hint

Do not confuse **transformation** with **translation**. A **translation** is a type of **transformation**.

1. What are the coordinates of the preimage?

   P_____ , Q_____ , R_____ , S_____

2. What are the coordinates of Hunter's image?

   P_____ , Q_____ , R_____ , S_____

3. What transformation was performed on the figure?

   _____

4. Yvonne's moves involved the following coordinates: P'(1, 4), Q'(5, 4), R'(7, −2), S'(3, −6). Draw and classify the transformed image.

   _____

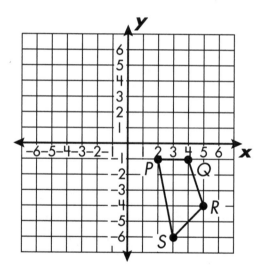

5. Taneshia's transformed image has points at (−4, −1), (−2, −1), (−5, −4), and (−3, −6). What type of transformation is this?

   _____

Check What You Learned

Geometry

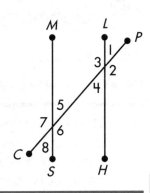

Read the problem carefully and solve. Show your work under each question.

The building committee presented the plans and blueprint for a new middle school to the principal, Mr. Avery. Mr. Avery is reviewing the plans in order to make suggestions before giving his approval. The figure on the right shows the hallways in an academic wing of the school.

1. Two hallways are parallel. Write their names using a symbol and letters.

   _____ and _____

2. Name the hallway that represents a transversal using a symbol and letters.

   _____

3. Mr. Avery highlights $\overline{PC}$ to represent the distance from his office (P) to the counselor's office (C). What does $\overline{PC}$ represent?

   _____

4. Which angles are obtuse?

   _____

5. Which angles are vertical angles?

   _____

   _____

6. Which angles are acute?

   _____

7. Which pairs of angles are alternate interior angles?

   _____

8. Which pairs of angles are alternate exterior angles?

   _____

9. $\angle 1$ measures 42°. What is the measure of $\angle 5$?

   _____

Check What You Learned

Geometry

Read the problem carefully and solve. Show your work under each question.

Mr. Avery is also looking at the plans for the soccer fields and outdoor grounds.

1. The sketch below shows the triangular area for a flowerbed. Name this triangle in two ways; one based on its angles, and one based on its sides.

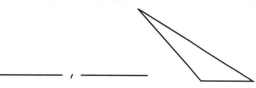

_____ , _____

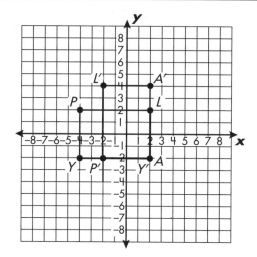

2. Mr. Avery decides that he would like to proportionally enlarge the triangular lobby outside the main office. The figures below show the original area and the enlarged area.

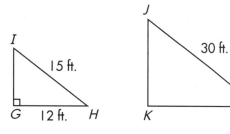

What is the length of $\overline{JK}$?

_____ feet

3. Mr. Avery does not like the placement of the soccer field. The figure above shows the original and updated placement of the field. What are the coordinates of the original placement of the field represented by points P, L, A, and Y?

P(_____) L(_____) A(_____) Y(_____)

4. What are the coordinates of the updated placement of the field represented by points P', L', A', and Y'?

P'(_____) L'(_____) A'(_____) Y'(_____)

5. What type of transformation was performed?

_____

Check What You Know

Perimeter, Area, and Volume

Read the problem carefully and solve. Show your work under each question.

Jonathan is submitting a project for the school Geography Fair. He uses a piece of presentation board to draw different shapes to represent parts of his ideal city.

1. What is the area of the presentation board?

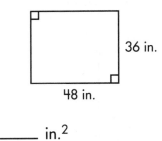

36 in.

48 in.

_____ in.²

2. To help it stand out, Jonathan paints the perimeter of the board a bright color. What is the perimeter of the presentation board?

_____ inches

3. Jonathan draws the triangle below to represent a park in his city. What is the area of the triangle he draws?

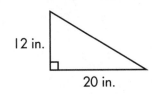

12 in.

20 in.

_____ in.²

4. The circle below is drawn to represent the city pond. What is the area of the circle?

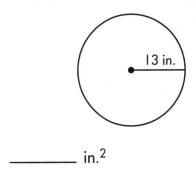

13 in.

_____ in.²

5. Jonathan highlights the edge of the circle to represent a walking trail. What is the length of the trail?

_____ inches

6. The figure below represents the area of the city park. What is the area of the figure?

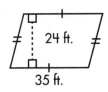

24 ft.

35 ft.

_____ ft.²

NAME _____

Check What You Know

Perimeter, Area, Volume

Read the problem carefully and solve. Show your work under each question.

Jonathan makes solid figures to represent various buildings in his city. For the presentation, he paints each figure and glues it to a piece of plywood.

1. Jonathan uses a rectangular solid to represent a building in his city. What is the surface area of the rectangular solid he makes?

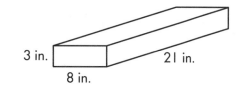

3 in.　21 in.

8 in.

_____ in.^{2}

2. What is the volume of the figure?

_____ in.^{3}

3. A cylindrical shape is used to represent the water tower in the town. What is the surface area of the cylinder Jonathan makes?

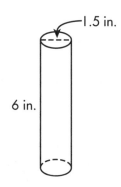

1.5 in.

6 in.

_____ in.^{2}

4. What is the volume of the cylinder?

_____ in.^{3}

5. Jonathan uses a cone shape to represent the gift shop. What is the surface area and volume of the cone he makes?

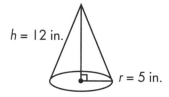

h = 12 in.　r = 5 in.

SA = _____ in.^{2}

V = _____ in.^{3}

6. A bank in Jonathan's city is represented by a pyramid. What is the surface area and volume of the pyramid he makes?

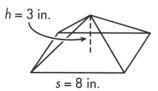

h = 3 in.

s = 8 in.

SA = _____ in.^{2}

V = _____ in.^{3}

Lesson 8.1 Perimeter

Read the problem carefully and solve. Show your work under each question.

Samaria helps her grandmother at her shop making custom table linens. Her job is to put fringe around the edges of different tablecloths.

Helpful Hint

If a polygon is **regular**, meaning that all sides are equal in length, you can multiply the length of one side by the number of sides.

1. A standard square tablecloth has the dimensions shown below. How much fringe does Samaria need for this perimeter?

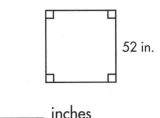

52 in.

_____ inches

2. How much fringe does Samaria need for a rectangular tablecloth that is 84 inches long and 60 inches wide?

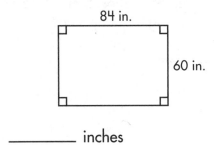

84 in.

60 in.

_____ inches

3. Samaria attached 165 inches of fringe material to a tablecloth. If the tablecloth was in the shape of a regular pentagon, how much fringe material did she use per side?

_____ inches

4. Samaria puts the fringe on a triangular tablecloth shown below. How much fringe does she need?

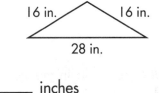

16 in.   16 in.

28 in.

_____ inches

5. Samaria's grandmother gets a special order for a tablecloth shaped like a regular hexagon. The sides of the hexagon measure 40 inches. How much fringe does Samaria need?

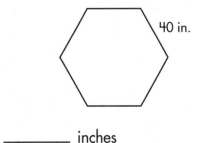

40 in.

_____ inches

Lesson 8.2 Area of a Rectangle

Read the problem carefully and solve. Show your work under each question.

Forrest works in a rug store. He is in charge of determining prices based on the areas of the rugs.

> **Helpful Hint**
>
> Area is expressed in **square units** or **units²**.

1. A kitchen rug sold in the store is 4 feet by 6 feet. What is the area of the rug?

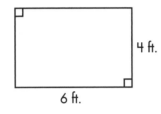

6 ft.

4 ft.

_____ ft.²

2. The smallest rug sold in the store is 3.5 feet by 4.5 feet. What is the area of the rug?

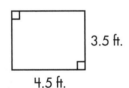

3.5 ft.

4.5 ft.

_____ ft.²

3. A square rug and a rectangular rug both have a perimeter of 16 feet. Which rug has the greater area, and what is the area?

_____ _____ ft.²

4. One of the larger rugs has a length of 14 feet and a width of 8 feet. What is the area of this rug?

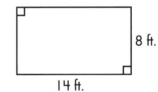

8 ft.

14 ft.

_____ ft.²

5. A square rug has an area of 72.25 ft². What is the length of one side?

_____ feet

Lesson 8.3 Area of a Triangle

Read the problem carefully and solve. Show your work under each question.

Myong gets a summer job mowing lawns for the department of public works. He estimates how long each lawn will take based on the area of the lawn.

Helpful Hint

Do not confuse the height of a triangle with a diagonal side.

$A = \frac{1}{2} bh$

1. The lawn in front of city hall is shaped like the figure below. What is the area?

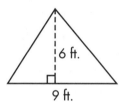

6 ft.

9 ft.

_____ ft.^{2}

2. The library's back yard has a picnic area shaped like the figure below. What is the area?

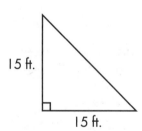

15 ft.

15 ft.

_____ ft.^{2}

3. The grassy area at the intersection of Main and South streets is shaped like the figure below. What is the area?

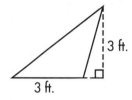

3 ft.

3 ft.

_____ ft.^{2}

4. The town green is shaped like the figure below. What is the area?

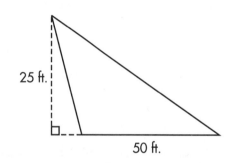

25 ft.

50 ft.

_____ ft.^{2}

5. The intersection of North Street and West Street forms the shape shown below, which is a grass field. The area of the shape is 405 ft.^{2}. What is the length of base?

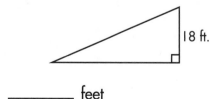

18 ft.

_____ feet

Lesson 8.4 Circumference of a Circle

Read the problem carefully and solve. Show your work under each question.

Amanda makes circular ceramic plates. She loves to add trim to the plates with bold colors.

> **Helpful Hint**
>
> The formula for finding circumference is πd or $2\pi r$. Be sure to use the correct value for each formula.
>
> Use 3.14 for π and round to the nearest hundredth.

1. A dinner plate has a diameter of 10.5 inches. What is the radius and circumference?

   radius _____ inches

   circumference _____ inches

2. The radius of a salad plate is 4.5 inches. What is the diameter and circumference?

   diameter _____ inches

   circumference _____ inches

3. A serving platter has a circumference of 37.68 inches. What is the radius?

   radius _____ inches

4. The diameter of a dessert plate is 7.5 inches. What is the radius and circumference?

   radius _____ inches

   circumference _____ inches

5. A saucer has a circumference of 20.41 inches. What is the diameter of the saucer?

   diameter _____ inches

Lesson 8.5 Area of a Circle

Read the problem carefully and solve. Show your work under each question.

Mariah is shopping for round tables for her patio. She needs to decide which size tables she thinks will look best on her porch.

Helpful Hint

The **area** of a circle is the number of square units it contains.

The formula for finding the area of a circle is:

Area = π × radius × radius

$A = \pi r^2$

Use 3.14 for π and round to the nearest hundredth.

1. A glass tabletop has a diameter of 34 inches. What is the radius and area?

radius _____ inches

area _____ in.^{2}

2. A plastic tabletop has a radius of 23 inches. What is the diameter and area?

diameter _____ inches

area _____ in.^{2}

3. The largest tabletop has a diameter of 72 inches. What is the radius and area?

radius _____ inches

area _____ in.^{2}

4. The smallest available table has a radius of 8 inches. What is the diameter and area?

diameter _____ inches

area _____ in.^{2}

5. Mariah chooses a table with an area of 1,519.76 in.^{2} because it will fit perfectly next to her door. What is the diameter of the table?

_____ inches

Lesson 8.6 Area of a Parallelogram

Read the problem carefully and solve. Show your work under each question.

Felipe is shopping for a sandbox to put in his backyard. The Sandcastle Summer Shop offers a number of sandboxes of various-sized parallelograms.

Helpful Hint

To find the **area** of a parallelogram, multiply the measure of its base by the measure of its height.

$A = b \times h$

$A = bh$

Do not confuse the height of a parallelogram with a diagonal side.

---

1. The first sandbox Felipe looked at is depicted below. What is the area of the sandbox?

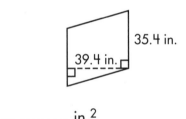

35.4 in.

39.4 in.

_____ in.²

2. What is the area of the sandbox depicted below?

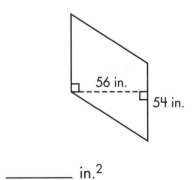

56 in.

54 in.

_____ in.²

3. The sandbox shown below has an area of 5,225 in.². What is the measurement depicted by the dashed line?

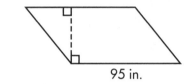

95 in.

_____ inches

4. What is the area of the sandbox depicted below?

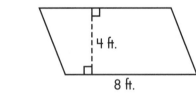

4 ft.

8 ft.

_____ ft.²

5. The area of the sandbox depicted below is 61.75 ft.². What is the length of the right edge?

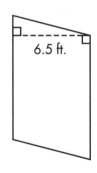

6.5 ft.

_____ feet

Lesson 8.7 Surface Area of a Rectangular Solid

Read the problem carefully and solve. Show your work under each question.

The local nursing home is planning a party. Reese has five different boxes to wrap. The boxes will contain gifts for the senior citizens.

Helpful Hint

The **surface area** of a solid is the sum of the areas of all surfaces of a solid.

A rectangular solid has 6 surfaces.

1. How many square inches of wrapping paper does Reese need to cover the box depicted below?

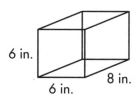

6 in.   6 in.   8 in.

_____ in.²

2. The box shown below will be used to hold Reese's grandmother's gift. How much wrapping paper is needed to cover this box?

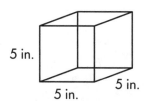

5 in.   5 in.   5 in.

_____ in.²

3. Reese also has a gift for her grandmother's friend. How much wrapping paper is needed to cover this box?

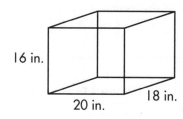

16 in.   20 in.   18 in.

_____ in.²

4. Reese wrapped the present shown below. What is the surface area of the present?

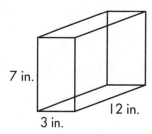

7 in.   3 in.   12 in.

_____ in.²

5. The largest box Reese wrapped is shown below. She did not cover the top of the box. How much wrapping paper did she use?

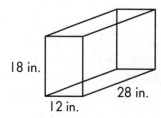

18 in.   12 in.   28 in.

_____ in.²

Lesson 8.8   Volume of a Rectangular Solid

Read the problem carefully and solve. Show your work under each question.

Keisha works at a pet store. She is in charge of repairing tanks and ordering filters for the tanks. She determines the type of filter to order for each tank based on the amount of water that the tank holds. Keisha knows that all of the tanks are rectangular solids.

Helpful Hint

Calculate the volume of a rectangular solid by multiplying the area of its base by its height: $V = Bh$. Use cubic units for volume.

1. What is the volume of the tank depicted below?

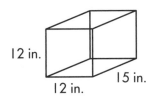

12 in.   12 in.   15 in.

_____ in.^{3}

2. What is the volume of the tank shown below?

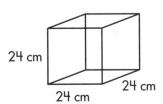

24 cm   24 cm   24 cm

_____ cm^3

3. Keisha has to order sealant to fix the vertical edges of a tank. She remembers that the tank has a volume of 5,760 in.^{3}, the width is 20 inches, and the length is 18 inches. How tall is the tank?

_____ inches

4. To clean the tank shown below, Keisha had to remove half of the water. How much water did Keisha remove?

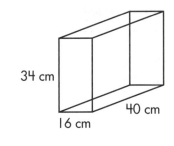

34 cm   16 cm   40 cm

_____ cm^3

5. What is the volume of the tank shown below?

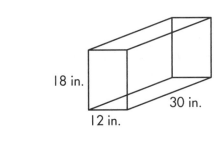

18 in.   12 in.   30 in.

_____ in.^{3}

Lesson 8.9 Surface Area of a Cylinder

Read the problem carefully and solve. Show your work under each question.

Fiona is shopping at the department store for some new pillows. She is interested in cylinder-shaped pillows. The pillows can be customized with different types of fabric. The cost of the pillows depends on the amount and type of fabric.

Helpful Hint

For a **cylinder**, the surface area is the area of the circles at the top and bottom, plus the area of the round section in the middle.

The surface area is found with the formula: $SA = 2(\pi r^2) + 2\pi rh$.

Surface area is expressed in **square units**.

Use 3.14 for π when calculating surface area.

1. A cowhide-pattern pillow has a diameter of 20 cm and a height of 10 cm. What is the surface area of the pillow?

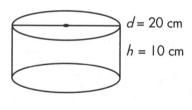

$d = 20$ cm
$h = 10$ cm

_____ cm²

2. An animal print pillow has a radius of 8 inches and a height of 50 inches. What is the surface area of the pillow?

_____ in.²

3. Fiona's favorite cylindrical pillow has a diameter of 6 inches and a height of 12 inches. What is the surface area of the pillow?

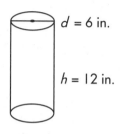

$d = 6$ in.

$h = 12$ in.

_____ in.²

4. A large pillow has a diameter of 2 feet and a height of 5 feet. Fiona wants to cover the curved part of the pillow with blue fabric and cover the circular ends with red fabric. How much blue fabric will be used?

_____ ft.²

5. A child's pillow is shown below. The pillow is green except for one circular end, which is a tiger-print fabric. How much green fabric is there? Round your answer to the nearest tenth of a square foot.

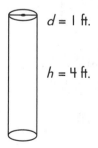

$d = 1$ ft.

$h = 4$ ft.

_____ ft.²

Lesson 8.10 Volume of a Cylinder

Read the problem carefully and solve. Show your work under each question.

Janelle is filling various size containers with potpourri. She will place the containers in various rooms within the house.

> **Helpful Hint**
>
> Calculate the **volume of a cylinder** by multiplying the area of the base by the height (*Bh*).
>
> Volume can be found using the formula: $V = \pi r^2 h$.
>
> Volume is expressed in **cubic units**, or **units**^{3}.

1. A container with diameter 8 cm and height 5 cm will be placed in the bathroom. How much potpourri will this container hold?

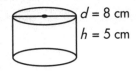

d = 8 cm
h = 5 cm

_____ cm^3

2. The container Janelle fills for the kitchen has a diameter of 2 inches and a height of 3.5 inches. How much potpourri is needed to fill this container?

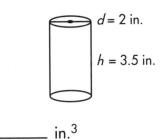

d = 2 in.

h = 3.5 in.

_____ in.^{3}

3. The living room will have a container with a radius of 4 centimeters and a height of 12 centimeters. How much potpourri will this container hold?

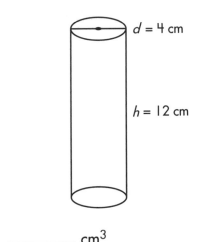

d = 4 cm

h = 12 cm

_____ cm^3

4. Janelle puts a small container in her linen closet. The container holds 37.68 in.^{3} of potpourri. If the diameter of the base is 4 inches, how tall is the container?

_____ inches

5. The container for the master bedroom is shown below. How much potpourri is needed for this container?

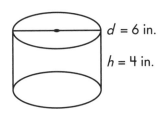

d = 6 in.

h = 4 in.

_____ in.^{3}

Lesson 8.11 Surface Area of a Cone

Read the problem carefully and solve. Show your work under each question.

The Happy Hat Company sells hats for various occasions. Mario helps determine the amount of materials that are needed to fill orders.

Helpful Hint

Surface area of a cone is the sum of the area of the base plus the area of the top portion of the cone.

$$SA = \pi r \ell + \pi r^2$$

Use 3.14 for π.

1. Birthday hats with a princess theme have a height of 8 centimeters and a diameter of 12 centimeters. What is the surface area of the hat?

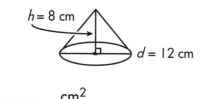

_____ cm^2

2. Hats decorated with farm animals have a radius of 5 inches and a height of 12 inches. What is the surface area of each hat?

_____ in.^{2}

3. Mario determines the measurements of birthday hats for dolls shown below. What is the surface area of each hat?

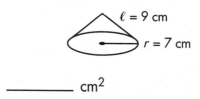

_____ cm^2

4. Safari birthday hats have a side length of 10 inches. What is the surface area of each hat?

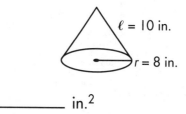

_____ in.^{2}

5. A large display hat has a diameter of 32 inches. What is the surface area of the hat?

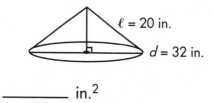

_____ in.^{2}

Lesson 8.12 Volume of a Cone

Read the problem carefully and solve. Show your work under each question.

A group of friends stop at the Healthy Fruit and Nut Company after school to buy some dried fruits and nuts. All sizes of fruits and nuts come in a cone-shaped container.

Helpful Hint

The **volume of a cone** is calculated as $\frac{1}{3}$ base × height.

$V = \frac{1}{3}\pi r^2 h$

Volume is given in **cubic units**, or **units³**.

Use 3.14 for π.

1. Davis buys a snack-size container of pecans. What is the volume of this container?

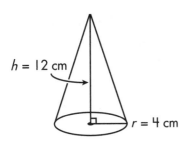

_____ cm³

2. Gabrielle likes dried cranberries. She purchases a small container. What is the volume of this container?

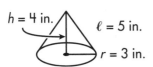

_____ in.³

3. Patsy will use her walnuts to bake muffins. She purchases a medium-size container, shown below. What is the volume?

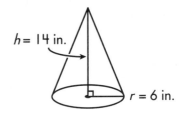

_____ in.³

4. Yasmin purchases the mixed dried-fruit assortment. She buys a large container that will hold enough of the snack, 2,190 in.³, to last many days. What is the height of the container?

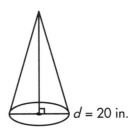

_____ inches

5. Evan buys an extra-large container of peanuts to share with his family. What is the volume of this container?

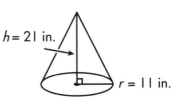

_____ in.³

Lesson 8.13 Surface Area of a Square Pyramid

Read the problem carefully and solve. Show your work under each question.

Whitney is in charge of painting model pyramids for the local museum. She needs to determine the amount of paint she'll need, based on the surface area of each square pyramid.

> **Helpful Hint**
>
> The **surface area of a square pyramid** is the sum of the area of the square side and each of the 4 triangular sides.
>
> $SA = s^2 + 2s\ell$
>
> SA is given in **square units**, or **units**^{2}.

3.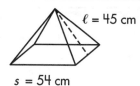

$\ell = 45$ cm

$s = 54$ cm

_____ cm^2

For questions 1–5, find the surface area of each pyramid. Round answers to the nearest hundredth.

1.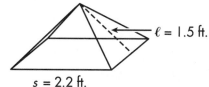

$\ell = 1.5$ ft.

$s = 2.2$ ft.

_____ ft.^{2}

4.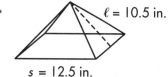

$\ell = 10.5$ in.

$s = 12.5$ in.

_____ in.^{2}

2.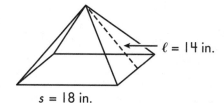

$\ell = 14$ in.

$s = 18$ in.

_____ in.^{2}

5.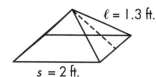

$\ell = 1.3$ ft.

$s = 2$ ft.

_____ ft.^{2}

Lesson 8.14 Volume of a Square Pyramid

Read the problem carefully and solve. Show your work under each question.

Kami will bring hand painted pyramids to the museum. She needs to determine the amount of space the pyramids will occupy in the delivery truck.

Helpful Hint

The **volume of a pyramid** is calculated as $\frac{1}{3}$ base × height.

$V = \frac{1}{3}Bh$ or $\frac{1}{3}s^2h$

Volume is given in **cubic units**, or **units^3**.

For questions 1–5, find the volume of each pyramid. Round answers to the nearest hundredth.

1. $h = 1.5$ ft.

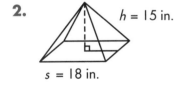

$s = 2.2$ ft.

_____ ft.^{3}

2.

$h = 15$ in.

$s = 18$ in.

_____ in.^{3}

3. $h = 15$ cm

$s = 24$ cm

_____ cm^3

4. $h = 10.5$ in.

$s = 12.5$ in.

_____ in.^{3}

5. $h = 1.3$ ft.

$s = 2$ ft.

_____ ft.^{3}

Check What You Learned

Perimeter, Area, and Volume

Read the problem carefully and solve. Show your work under each question.

A group of friends spends a Saturday afternoon at the city park. They plan to explore the park and participate in various activities. They will swim, bike, play basketball, and take the time to have a snack.

1. The city park measures 2 miles by 4.5 miles. What is the area of the park?

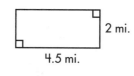

_____ mi.^{2}

2. What is the perimeter of the park?

_____ miles

3. A triangular area is roped off for children to play hopscotch or to jump rope. What is the area of this triangular region?

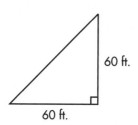

_____ ft.^{2}

4. Another area is fenced off for basketball courts and tennis courts. What is the area of this region?

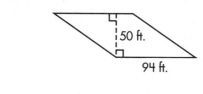

_____ ft.^{2}

5. Some students spend time swimming in the circular pond. The pond has a radius of 1.5 km. What is the area of the pond?

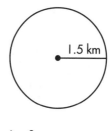

_____ km^2

6. A bike trail encircles the pond. How far do the students ride if they bike around the entire pond?

_____ km

7. Parts of the park benches are made of pieces of cylindrical steel. One piece has a diameter of 6 inches and a height of 15 inches. What are the surface area and volume of the piece?

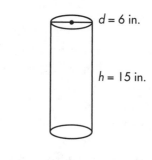

_____ in.^{2}

_____ in.^{3}

Check What You Learned

Perimeter, Area, Volume

Read the problem carefully and solve. Show your work under each question.

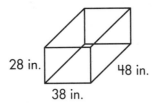

28 in.   48 in.

38 in.

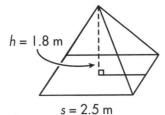

$h = 1.8$ m

$s = 2.5$ m

8. The friends order yogurt cones from the snack cart. The cart is covered with colorful pictures of the park. It measures 48 inches wide, 38 inches long, and 28 inches high. What is the surface area of the cart?

_____ in.^{2}

9. What is the volume of the cart?

_____ in.^{3}

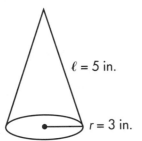

$\ell = 5$ in.

$r = 3$ in.

10. Javier orders a strawberry cheesecake waffle cone. The cone has a radius of 3 inches and a side length of 5 inches. What is the surface area of the cone?

_____ in.^{2}

11. What is the volume of the cone?

_____ in.^{3}

12. The park has a special decorative sculpture shaped like a square pyramid at the entrance. The sculpture measures 2.5 meters on one side, is 1.8 meters tall, and has a slant height of 1.3 meters. What is the surface area of the sculpture?

_____ m^2

13. What is the volume of the sculpture?

_____ m^3

Check What You Know

Preparing for Algebra

Read the problem carefully and solve. Show your work under each question.

Eighth-grade math teacher, Mrs. Pascal, attends a national math conference. She visits the various vendor booths and stops at a new booth that offers a variety of new math games. Mrs. Pascal reads the back of the boxes of the games to get an idea of what the game is and if it is appropriate for her students.

1. "Power Up" is the first game that Mrs. Pascal considers. Solve the tasks below.

   a. Rewrite each expression using a base and an exponent.

   $7^3 \times 7^2 =$ _____

   $12^{-6} \times 12^{-4} =$ _____

   b. Write 1,952 in scientific notation.

   _____

   c. Write 1.974×10^{-5} in standard notation.

   _____

2. Mrs. Pascal looks at a game called "Who Am I?" It involves variables, equations, and inequalities. Solve the problems from the game below.

   a. Write "a number times 6 plus 9" as an algebraic expression.

   _____

   b. Write "a number less than 14 is 6" as an equation.

   _____

3. The game "Attributes and Properties" has many examples listed on the back of the box. Write an equation to illustrate each property.

   a. The Commutative Property of Addition

   _____

   b. The Distributive Property

   _____

4. "Mystery Math" is Mrs. Pascal's favorite game. It involves solving various equations. Solve each problem by writing a variable equation.

   a. Carlos saved $450. This is 15 times the amount that Emma saved. How much money did Emma save?

   Equation: _____

   $n =$ _____

   b. Michelle bought 2 blouses and a skirt. The skirt cost $14 and Michelle spent a total of $32. What is the cost of 1 blouse?

   Equation: _____

   $n =$ _____

Lesson 9.1 Multiplying and Dividing Powers

Read the problem carefully and solve. Show your work under each question.

Scott is the supply clerk for a small business office. He is responsible for ordering supplies and delivering them to employees as needed. Scott takes inventory and finds that he needs to order pens, index cards, rubber bands, staples, and paper clips.

Helpful Hint

$4^2 \times 4^3 = (4 \times 4) \times (4 \times 4 \times 4)$

I. Staples come 10^2 per box and 10^3 boxes per case. Write the expression for the total number of staples in one case using a base and an exponent.

_____

2. Index cards come 5^2 per box and 5^4 per case. Write the expression for the total number of index cards in one case using a base and an exponent.

_____

3. There are 3^5 pens per case. Each box contains 3^2 pens. Write the expression for the number of boxes in each case using a base and an exponent.

_____

4. Rubber bands come 2^5 per box and 2^{10} per case. Write the expression for the total number of rubber bands in one case using a base and an exponent.

_____

5. A case of paper clips contains 10^6 clips. One box contains 10^2 paper clips. Write the expression for the number of boxes in each case using a base and an exponent.

_____

Lesson 9.2 Negative Exponents

Read the problem carefully and solve. Show your work under each question.

Before he starts teaching a new unit, Mr. Sanchez gives the students a pretest to assess how much time he will have to spend reviewing this concept with his students.

Helpful Hint

$3^{-4} = \frac{1}{3^4} = \frac{1}{81}$

1. Rewrite $4^{-3} \times 4^{-2}$ using a base and an exponent.

_____

2. Rewrite $5^{-15} \div 5^{-6}$ using a base and an exponent.

_____

3. Rewrite $8^{-6} \times 8^3$ using a base and an exponent.

_____

4. Rewrite $9^2 \div 9^{-8}$ using a base and an exponent.

_____

5. How would you write 100 divided by $\frac{1}{100}$ using a base of 10 and two different exponents?

_____

NAME _____

Lesson 9.3 Scientific Notation

Read the problem carefully and solve. Show your work under each question.

The eighth-grade science class visits a display at the local science museum. The display gives information about the solar system. It also includes a model of the planets revolving around the sun.

Helpful Hint

Negative exponents in scientific notation move the decimal to the left.

1. Juan reads that Mercury is the closest planet to the sun. It is approximately 58,000,000 km from the sun. Write this number in scientific notation.

_____ km

2. Juan continues reading and finds that Jupiter is approximately 7.785×10^8 km from the sun. Write this number in standard form.

_____ km

3. By observation, Alicia concludes that Jupiter is the largest planet. She reads that Jupiter's diameter is 142,800 km. Write this number in scientific notation.

_____ km

4. Chloe uses a scale to weigh a moon rock. She finds that it weighs 0.0746 kg. Write this number in scientific notation.

_____ kg

5. Orlando chooses to weigh a different moon rock and finds that it weighs 8.34×10^{-1} kg. Write this number in standard form.

_____ kg

Lesson 9.4 Variables, Equations, and Inequalities

Read the problem carefully and solve. Show your work under each question.

Stephen likes to play games and riddles with his family. At dinnertime, he often likes to quiz each family member. Stephen learned about variables and expressions in Math class and uses this knowledge for a new round of riddles.

> **Helpful Hint**
>
> A **variable** is a letter that stands for an unknown number.

1. Stephen tells his mom that her age is 3 times his age. Use *a* to represent Stephen's age and write the expression to show his mother's age.

_____

2. "I'm 8 years older than my baby sister, Caroline," says Stephen. Use *s* to represent Stephen's sister's age and write the expression.

_____

3. "Two times my age is greater than 20." Translate this phrase into an algebraic inequality.

_____

4. "Twice my age divided by 4 is 6." Translate this phrase into an algebraic equation.

_____

5. "My age minus 3 equals 15." Translate this phrase into an algebraic equation.

_____

Lesson 9.5 Order of Operations

Read the problem carefully and solve. Show your work under each question.

Mrs. Perez is correcting a Math quiz. She finds recurring errors and will use these examples to re-teach the order of operations during the next class.

> **Helpful Hint**
>
> Perform multiplication and division in the same step.
>
> Perform addition and subtraction in the same step.

1. Simplify $30 - 7 + (12 + 15 \div 3)$.

_____

2. Simplify $6 \times 3 \div 9 \times 8 + 4^2$.

_____

3. Evaluate $ab^2 - 2a \div 4$ if $a = 6$ and $b = 5$.

_____

4. Evaluate $90 \div x^2 + (2y - 5)$ if $x = 3$ and $y = 8$.

_____

5. Zaina simplified $3 \times 6 + 4$, and her answer was 30. What error did she make? What is the correct answer?

_____

_____

Lesson 9.6 Number Properties

Read the problem carefully and solve. Show your work under each question.

Wynona is making flash cards to help her study the number properties. She writes the names of the properties on one side of the cards. On the other side of the cards, she writes an example. Help Wynona complete the cards by completing the equations below using your knowledge of number properties.

Helpful Hint

Commutative Properties of Addition and Multiplication:

$a + b = b + a \qquad a \times b = b \times a$

Associative Properties of Addition and Multiplication:

$(a + b) + c = a + (b + c)$
$(a \times b) \times c = a \times (b \times c)$

Identity Properties of Addition, Multiplication, and Exponents:

$a + 0 = a \qquad a \times 1 = a \qquad a^1 = a$

Properties of Zero:

$a \times 0 = 0 \qquad 0 \div a = 0$
$a^0 = 1$ unless $a = 0$

1. $p \times q = $ _____

2. $0 \div 5 = $ _____ 0

3. Which property of addition does $x + (y + z) = (x + y) + z$ show?

_____

4. Wynona practices solving equations using her knowledge of number properties. What is $5 \times (3 + 5)^0$?

_____

5. What does $(12 + 15)^0$ equal?

_____

Lesson 9.7 The Distributive Property

Read the problem carefully and solve. Show your work under each question.

Alfonso makes deliveries for the Office Plus Supply Company. His deliveries this week include computer ribbons, blank recordable CDs, toner for photocopy machines, file folders, and copy paper.

Helpful Hint

Distributive Property:

$a \times (b + c) = (a \times b) + (a \times c)$
$a \times (b - c) = (a \times b) - (a \times c)$

1. On Monday, Alfonso delivers 40 cases of duplicating paper and 2 cases of CDs to each of 30 different businesses. Use the Distributive Property to rewrite 42×30 in a way that will solve how many cases were delivered. Then, solve the problem.

   _____

   _____

2. His deliveries on Tuesday include stopping at 2 branches of insurance company a and 3 branches of bank b. He delivers 15 cases of computer ribbons to each of these businesses. Use the Distributive Property to rewrite $15(a + b)$.

   _____

3. Wednesday's task is to deliver 20 cases of toner to each of 15 different businesses. Use the Distributive Property to rewrite 20×15 in a way that will solve how many cases were delivered. Then, solve the problem.

   _____

   _____

4. On Thursday morning, Alfonso delivers 16 cases of blank recordable CDs to 30 businesses. In the afternoon, he delivers 16 cases of blank recordable CDs to 20 businesses. Use the Distributive Property to rewrite $(16 \times 30) + (16 \times 20)$ in a way that will solve how many cases were delivered. Then, solve the problem.

   _____

   _____

5. Alfonso delivers 10 cases of file folders to 2 town halls, t, on Friday morning. In the afternoon, Alfonso delivers 10 cases of file folders to high school s. Use the Distributive Property to rewrite $10t + 10s$.

   _____

Lesson 9.8 Solving Addition and Subtraction Equations

Read the problem carefully and solve. Show your work under each question.

> **Helpful Hint**
>
> Add or subtract the same amount from both sides of an equation to solve.

A group of people each wins $100 for a shopping spree at their favorite store.

1. Brad buys a pair of sneakers for $65 and a new shirt. He spends a total of $84. How much did he pay for the shirt? Write an equation using n to represent the shirt, and solve for the unknown number.

Equation: _____

$n =$ _____

2. Courtney spends $13 less than Nikki spends. If Courtney spends $56, how much does Nikki spend? Write an equation using x to represent the amount Nikki spends, and solve for the unknown number.

Equation: _____

$x =$ _____

3. Tiffany buys a blouse, skirt, and socks for $64. This is $9 more than Javier spends. How much does Javier spend? Write an equation using j to represent the amount Javier spends, and solve for the unknown number.

Equation: _____

$j =$ _____

4. Shelby spends $47. This is $21 less than what Porchia spends. How much money does Porchia spend? Write an equation using p to represent the amount Porchia spends, and solve for the unknown number.

Equation: _____

$p =$ _____

5. Courtney spends a total of $56 on a new dress and shoes. If the dress costs $35, how much do the shoes cost? Write the equation and solve for the unknown number.

Equation: _____

$n =$ _____

Lesson 9.9 Solving Multiplication and Division Equations

Read the problem carefully and solve. Show your work under each question.

Heather is making a quilt. She buys a number of pieces of fabric in different colors at the Crazy Quilt Shop. She then cuts the fabric into different lengths to use for her quilt.

Helpful Hint

Multiply or divide each side of an equation by the same amount to solve.

1. Heather buys 12 feet of the blue fabric. She wants to cut it into 4 pieces. How many feet will each piece be? Write an equation using f to represent the number of feet per piece, and solve for the unknown number.

   Equation: _____

   $f =$ _____

2. Heather has pieces of green fabric measuring 6 feet each. She cuts them from a piece that measures 30 feet. How many pieces of green fabric does she have? Write an equation using n to represent the number of pieces, and solve for the unknown number.

   Equation: _____

   $n =$ _____

3. Heather cuts a piece of red fabric into 4 pieces that are each 5 feet long. What is the length of the original piece of fabric? Write an equation using n to represent the length of the original piece, and solve for the unknown number.

   Equation: _____

   $n =$ _____

4. Each piece of yellow fabric is 8 inches long. If there are 12 pieces of yellow fabric, how many total inches of yellow fabric are there? Write an equation using n to represent the total length, and solve for the unknown number.

   Equation: _____

   $n =$ _____

5. There are 3 pieces of white fabric after Heather is finished cutting. Each piece is 8 feet long. What is the original length of the white fabric? Write the equation using l to represent the original length, and solve for the unknown number.

   Equation: _____

   $l =$ _____

Lesson 9.10 Solving Two-Step Equations

Read the problem carefully and solve. Show your work under each question.

The Kaplan family takes a trip to the nature center. They attend a special show and take the time to have lunch.

Helpful Hint

When solving 2-step equations, it is often easier to address addition and subtraction first.

1. Admission costs $13. The cost for Mr. Kaplan's admission plus 2 drinks can be represented by the equation $2d + 13 = 16$, where d represents the cost per drink. How much did each drink cost?

   _____

2. Mr. Kaplan has a coupon for $20 off of any show at the zoo. The total cost for the Kaplan family to attend a seal show can be represented by the equation $8m - 20 = 36$, where m represents the number of family members. How many members of the Kaplan family attended the seal show?

   _____

3. Four members of the family have lunch at the buffet. What is the total cost of lunch, not including the tip, if one meal plus a $3 tip equals $8?

   _____

4. Three of the children decide to eat lunch at the Healthy Snack Shack. They purchase three specials and each leave a tip of $2.50, represented by the equation $\frac{x}{3} + 2.50 = 11.50$. If they each spend $11.50, what was the total cost of the lunch before the tips?

   _____

5. The children buy souvenirs for their 4 grandparents. They spend $35, which includes a discount coupon for $5 off the entire purchase. If each souvenir costs the same, what is the price for one souvenir?

   _____

Lesson 9.11 Plotting Ordered Pairs

Read the problem carefully and solve. Show your work under each question.

Three friends play a game using the game board at the right. The object of the game is to guess where points are plotted on a coordinate plane. Jarred decided if the guesses were correct.

Grid 1

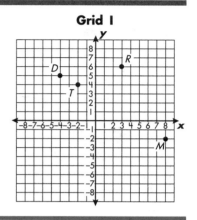

Helpful Hint

Points on a grid are located based on their (x, y) coordinates. The horizontal number is x and the vertical number is y. Point A on the grid below is at $(3, 2)$ which is 3 to the right and 2 up from the origin. Point B is at $(7, 3)$.

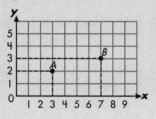

1. Alfonso correctly guessed where point T is located on the game board. What coordinates did Alfonso guess?

   $T ($ _____ $)$

2. Beth correctly guessed where point M is located on the game board. What coordinates did Beth guess?

   $M ($ _____ $)$

3. Jarred decided they should add some points to extend the game. He wants to plot point C, located at $(0, 7)$, point G, located at $(-5, 2)$, and point J, located at $(6, 3)$. Plot the ordered pair on the grid below.

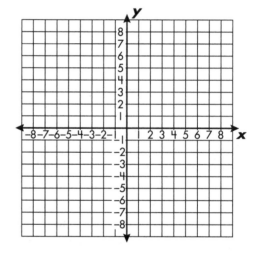

4. For the bonus round, Jarred asked what shape would result if the following points were plotted and lines were drawn to connect W to X, X to Y, Y to Z, and Z to W.

   $W (-7, -2)$, $X (-4, 3)$, $Y (5, 3)$ and $Z (2, -2)$.

   What is the shape?

   _____

Lesson 9.12 Creating Function Tables

Read the problem carefully and solve. Show your work under each question.

Three friends are practicing functions after school. Braden says, "Take a number and add four." Rachel says, "Take a number, multiply it by three, and subtract 5." Victor says, "Take a number, square it, then divide by three."

> **Helpful Hint**
>
> It's important to include negative x-values and 0 to show the full range of a function.

1. Braden's equation is represented by the function, $y = x + 4$. Complete a function table for this function.

$y = x + 4$

x	y
−3	1
−2	2
−1	
0	
3	

2. Rachel's equation is represented by the function, $y = 3x - 5$. Complete the function table for this function. Use the x-values −2, −1, 0, 1, and 2 for x.

$y = 3x - 5$

x	y

3. How is Victor's function written?

_____

4. Complete a function table for Victor's function using the x-values −6, −3, 0, 3, and 6.

x	y

5. Carter presents the function table below to the group. Identify the function this table represents.

x	y
−2	5
−1	2
0	1
1	2
2	5

$y =$ _____

Lesson 9.13 Graphing Linear Equations

Read the problem carefully and solve. Show your work under each question.

Perry works at the hot dog stand at the playground. He is asked to graph certain relationships between costs and expenses.

Helpful Hint

Remember that the first number in a coordinate pair is the x-value.

1. Perry is asked to graph the equation $y = x + 1$. Complete the function table. Then, graph the function.

x	y
1	
2	
4	
6	

3. The equation $y = 2x - 3$ shows the relationship between the expected number of customers and the number of condiments that should be ordered. Complete the function table. Then, graph the function.

x	y
1	
2	
3	
4	

2. Perry wants to graph the equation $y = x - 2$. Complete the function table. Then, graph the function.

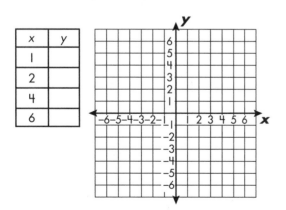

x	y
1	
2	
4	
6	

4. The equation $y = \frac{x}{2} + 1$ relates the amount of soda to the number of cups that are needed. Complete the function table. Then, graph the function.

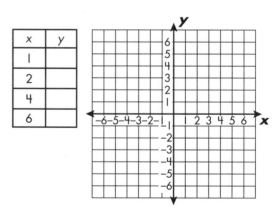

x	y
1	
2	
4	
6	

Check What You Learned

Preparing for Algebra

Read the problem carefully and solve. Show your work under each question.

Mrs. Pascal wants her students to write some problems that can be used as a review for a unit test.

1. Benji is assigned the section of powers. He writes the following problems. Solve Benji's problems.

   a. Rewrite each expression using a base and an exponent.

   $9^8 \div 9^5 =$ _____ $3^{-8} \times 3^{-5} =$ _____

   b. What is 2^{-4}? _____

   c. Write 3.4×10^6 in standard notation.

   _____

2. Garrett writes problems about variables, expressions, equations, and inequalities. Solve Garrett's problems.

   a. Translate "a number that is greater than 13" into an inequality.

   _____

   b. Translate "17 increased by the product of a number and 11 equals 50" into an equation.

   _____

3. Madison is assigned problems about number properties. Which property is illustrated by:

   $5 \times (8 \times 2) = (5 \times 8) \times 2$

   _____

4. "Solving Equations" is Owen's assignment. Solve Owen's problems.

   a. Stephanie is 5 years younger than Brantley. If Stephanie is 14, how old is Brantley?

   Equation: _____ $n =$ _____

   b. Cole bought 3 books and a DVD. The DVD cost $12 and Cole spent a total of $42. What is the cost of 1 book?

   Equation: _____ $n =$ _____

5. Rashad wrote the expression $(3 + 5 + 8) \times 4 - 52$. Simplify Rashad's expression.

   _____

6. Carrie makes a function table for $y = 4 - 2x$. Use the points, $-2, -1, 0, 1$ for x. Then, graph the function.

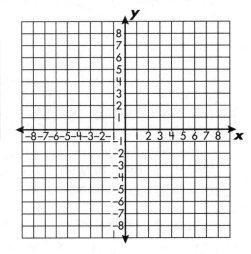

x	y
−2	
−1	
0	
1	

Final Test   Chapters 1–9

Read the problem carefully and solve. Show your work under each question.

Mr. Lopez registered 6 of his math students to participate in a state game board competition. They will travel with students and teachers from a neighboring school and will share all transportation costs.

---

1. Mr. Lopez pays $87 to cover 6 registrations and the processing fee. If each registration costs $12, how much was the processing fee? Write and solve an equation to represent the situation.

Equation: _____

n = _____

2. The van driver submits a bill for $194.70. This includes the cost of gas and a fee of $150 for the rental of the van.

a) How much was spent on gas?

_____

b) If gas costs $2.98 per gallon, how many gallons of gas did the van use?

_____ gallons

c) How much did each school pay for transportation?

_____

3. Mr. Lopez suggests that they make a mixture of walnuts and raisins. The students make 48 ounces of the mixture that is $\frac{3}{8}$ raisins. How many ounces of raisins are in the mixture?

_____ ounces

4. During the first round, Bridget and her opponent had a combined score of 21 points. Bridget scored 3 more points than her opponent. How many points did each student score? Write and solve an equation to represent the situation. Let *n* stand for the Bridget's score.

Equation: _____

Bridget's score: _____ points

Opponent's score: _____ points

5. Each team will compete in 6 rounds of 6 different games. Rewrite 6 × 6 as an expression using a base and an exponent.

_____

6. After the first round, Mr. Lopez made a bar graph showing how many points each of his students scored.

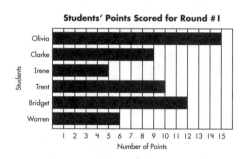

Students' Points Scored for Round #1

a) How many points did the team score during the first round?

_____ points

b) Who scored three times as many points as Irene? _____

Final Test Chapters 1–9

Read the problem carefully and solve. Show your work under each question.

The Real Estate game the students will play is made up of 40 spaces. There is a library, school, utility company, town hall, 4 banks, and 22 neighborhoods spread out over the 40 spaces.

1. The game board is 19.5 inches long and 19 inches wide. What is the area and perimeter of the game board?

   _____ in.²

   _____ inches

2. The game piece that represents a resort is shaped like a square pyramid. The length of the side of the base is 2 centimeters, the height is 1 centimeter, and the slant height is 1.5 centimeters. What is the surface area and the volume of the pyramid? Use 3.14 for π and round to the nearest hundredth.

   _____ cm²

   _____ cm³

3. The game piece that represents a water tower is shaped like a cylinder. It has a diameter of 1.6 centimeters and a height of 2.5 centimeters. What is the surface area and volume of the water tower piece? Use 3.14 for π and round to the nearest hundredth.

   _____ in.²

   _____ in.³

4. If there are 40 spaces on the game board, what is the probability of landing on a neighborhood or a bank? Write this number as a fraction in lowest terms, a decimal, and a percent.

   _____ _____ _____

5. The line plot shows the values of the properties.

   Assessed Value of Neighborhood Properties

   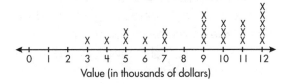

   Value (in thousands of dollars)

   a) What is the mode? What is the range?

   _____

   b) What is the mean and median?

   _____

6. It will cost the students $600 to put 4 houses in the neighborhoods. How much will it cost to build 11 houses?

   _____

Final Test Chapters 1–9

Read the problem carefully and solve. Show your work under each question.

Olivia, Clarke, Irene, Trent, Bridget, and Warren play the Real Estate game during round 2 of the competition. Each student is presented a different challenge.

1. Bridget lands on the school space and is asked to answer a chemistry question. The students at the school are working with chemicals, and they have to add 2^{-3} grams of a chemical to 2^5 beakers. Bridget needs to write the expression $2^{-3} \times 2^5$ using a base and an exponent. What is Bridget's answer?

   _____

2. Trent stops at Bank A. The bank offers simple interest of 4% on all savings accounts. Trent decides to put $600 of his money into the account for 3 rounds (years). How much money will he have after the 3 rounds?

   _____

3. Olivia and Warren get to work together when they each stop at Bank C. They each open an account with $500. Both accounts earn 2.5% interest. Olivia's account is compounded annually, and Warren's account is compounded semi-annually. How much more will Warren's account earn over 4 rounds (years)? Round to the nearest hundredth.

   _____

4. Clarke stops at the town hall. Clarke's challenge is to find out the area of grass that needs to be mowed in front of town hall. The patch is shaped like a right triangle and is 6 feet long and 4.5 feet wide. What is the area of the triangle?

   _____ ft.²

5. Irene stops at the stock exchange. She is given a function that relates the cost of a stock with the profit. She makes a function table and then graphs the function for the given function $y = 2x - 3$. Complete the function table and graph.

   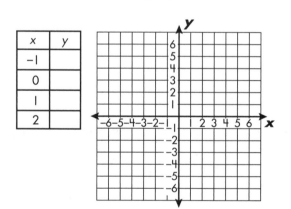

x	y
−1	
0	
1	
2	

Final Test Chapters 1–9

Read the problem carefully and solve. Show your work under each question.

The students play the game "Euclid's Challenge" during the third round of the competition. The game board is displayed on the right. Students will answer various questions about a number of topics in geometry.

Grid I

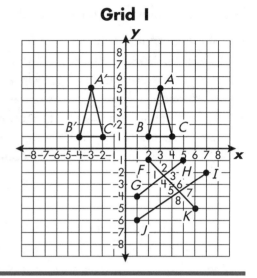

1. Label ΔABC in Quadrant I based on its angles and side lengths.

   _____

2. Refer to ΔABC in Quadrant I to answer the following questions.

   a) What are the coordinates of the preimage?

   A (_____), B (_____), C (_____)

   b) What are the coordinates of the image?

   A' (_____), B' (_____), C' (_____)

   c) What transformation was performed on ΔABC?

   _____

3. ΔABC has a base of 2 units and a height of 4 units. What is the base of a similar triangle with a height of 7 units?

   _____ units

   Refer to the drawing in Quadrant IV to answer numbers 4 and 5.

4. Which pairs of angles are vertical angles?

   _____

5. Which pairs of angles are alternate interior angles?

   _____

6. Name the two figures that make up ∠XYZ using a geometric symbol and letters.

   _____

Final Test Chapters 1–9

Read the problem carefully and solve. Show your work under each question.

The students at the Reagan Elementary School are excited to hear that the circus is coming to town. There will be several shows held at the local arena. Circus organizers will hold a special discounted show for the fourth and fifth graders.

1. Tickets sell for $15 each. Discount tickets for the elementary students are $12 each. What is the percent of the discount?

_____

2. The arena where the circus shows will be held has seats in three sections. The balcony has 9,880 seats, the mezzanine section has 6,125 seats, and the section on the floor can seat 3,575. What is the total capacity of the venue? What is this number in scientific notation?

_____ seats; _____

3. The balcony is divided evenly into sections that can seat 1,235 people. How many sections does the balcony have? Let n stand for the number of sections.

Equation: _____

$n =$ _____

4. The first act of the circus show is scheduled for $1\frac{1}{4}$ hours. There will be a $\frac{1}{2}$ hour intermission, and the second act will last $2\frac{1}{6}$ hours. How many total hours will the circus show be? What is this time in minutes?

_____ hours; _____ minutes

5. On the first day of the circus shows, the attendance of the evening performance was twice the attendance plus 45 of the matinee performance. Translate this phrase into an algebraic expression.

_____

6. The histogram below shows the circus revenues for 5 years.

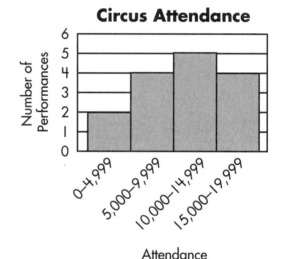

Circus Attendance

a) Which attendance range happened most often?

_____

b) How many total performances were there?

_____

Final Test Chapters 1–9

Read the problem carefully and solve. Show your work under each question.

The students enjoyed the high wire acts. They also enjoyed watching the elephants perform. The favorite acts were those involving clowns. The students loved watching the clowns make balloon animals at intermission.

1. One of the circus rings has a diameter of 120 meters. What is the area of the ring? What is the circumference of the ring?

   _____ m^2

   _____ meters

2. The high wire platform is 36 feet above ground. A ladder is placed 15 feet from the bottom of the platform. How long is the ladder?

   _____ feet

3. During one of the clown acts, a clown falls into a tub of water that holds 208.12 liters. How many kiloliters is this?

   _____ kiloliter

4. During the elephant act, an elephant placed one leg on a rectangular solid. The solid measures 12 inches by 16 inches by 18 inches. What is the surface area and volume of the solid?

   _____ in.^{2}

   _____ in.^{3}

5. The elephant picks up a weight that is labeled 42 kilograms. How many grams is this?

   _____ grams

6. During the intermission, the circus clowns entertain the children by making balloon animals. The children can choose either a red, blue, green, or yellow balloon. They can request that the clown make a dog, mouse, or giraffe balloon. How many different combinations of balloon animals can a child choose from? Make a tree diagram to solve.

   _____

Scoring Record for Posttests, Mid-Test, and Final Test

Chapter Posttest	Your Score	Performance			
		Excellent	Very Good	Fair	Needs Improvement
1	____ of 6	6	5	3–4	2 or fewer
2	____ of 6	6	5	3–4	2 or fewer
3	____ of 6	6	5	3–4	2 or fewer
4	____ of 6	6	5	3–4	2 or fewer
5	____ of 6	6	5	3–4	2 or fewer
6	____ of 20	20	17–19	13–16	12 or fewer
7	____ of 14	13–14	10–12	7–9	6 or fewer
8	____ of 13	12–13	10–11	7–9	6 or fewer
9	____ of 6	6	5	3–4	2 or fewer
Mid-Test	____ of 24	22–24	20–21	16–19	15 or fewer
Final Test	____ of 35	32–35	28–31	23–27	22 or fewer

Record your test score in the Your Score column. See where your score falls in the Performance columns. Your score is based on the total number of required responses. If your score is fair or needs improvement, review the chapter material.

Grade 8 Answers

Chapter 1

Pretest, page 1
1. 1,011
2. $15\frac{11}{12}$
3. $52.04
4. $1\frac{1}{15}$
5. $44.50
6. 33.7

Lesson 1.1, page 2
1. 6,765
2. 2,948
3. 3,428
4. 1,536
5. 4,352

Lesson 1.2, page 3
1. 75,028
2. 34,123
3. 104,946
4. 66,169
5. 58,144

Lesson 1.3, page 4
1. 36,419
2. 46,844
3. 25,970
4. 96,773
5. 117,020

Lesson 1.4, page 5
1. 52; 4
2. 214; 0
3. 963; 2
4. 12; 2,635
5. 250; 666; 4

Lesson 1.5, page 6
1. $10,124.60
2. $1,374.60
3. $4,150.00
4. $5,499.61
5. $1,349.61

Lesson 1.6, page 7
1. $8.72
2. $13.70
3. $11.97
4. $11.44
5. $11.62

Lesson 1.7, page 8
1. 152
2. 15
3. $12.45
4. $7.50
5. $23.75

Lesson 1.8, page 9
1. $\frac{1}{5}$
2. $\frac{1}{3}$
3. $\frac{3}{17}$
4. $\frac{3}{19}$
5. $2\frac{1}{3}$

Lesson 1.9, page 10
1. $3\frac{3}{4}$
2. $4\frac{1}{2}$
3. $1\frac{1}{4}$
4. $\frac{47}{7}$
5. $\frac{17}{2}$

Lesson 1.10, page 11
1. $5\frac{11}{40}$
2. $5\frac{5}{24}$
3. $10\frac{3}{4}$
4. $3\frac{5}{12}$
5. $3\frac{1}{40}$

Lesson 1.11, page 12
1. $4\frac{3}{8}$
2. $1\frac{7}{8}$
3. $3\frac{3}{4}$
4. $1\frac{1}{12}$
5. $\frac{13}{16}$

Lesson 1.12, page 13
1. 10
2. 4
3. 6
4. 4
5. 6

Posttest, page 14
1. 11
2. 77
3. $89.21
4. 40
5. 21
6. 19.85

Chapter 2

Pretest, page 15
1. 75
2. 54
3. 29
4. 8
5. 40
6. 6

Grade 8 Answers

Lesson 2.1, page 16
1. no, $\frac{1}{4} \neq \frac{15}{64}$
2. yes, $\frac{3}{8} = \frac{54}{144}$
3. yes, $\frac{27}{144} = \frac{12}{64}$
4. no, $\frac{35}{75} \neq \frac{45}{85}$
5. yes, $\frac{17}{85} = \frac{15}{75}$

Lesson 2.2, page 17
1. 72
2. 33.75
3. 250
4. 9
5. 27

Posttest, page 18
1. 70
2. 133
3. $96.00
4. 24
5. $161
6. $6.02

Chapter 3

Pretest, page 19
1. 0.35 and $\frac{7}{20}$
2. 33
3. 30%
4. 105
5. $1,440
6. $2,459.22

Lesson 3.1, page 20
1. 0.24 and $\frac{6}{25}$
2. 0.09 and $\frac{9}{100}$
3. 0.36 and $\frac{9}{25}$
4. 1.05 and $1\frac{1}{20}$
5. 1.25 and $1\frac{1}{4}$

Lesson 3.2, page 21
1. $\frac{3}{20}$
2. 12.5%
3. 40%
4. $1\frac{1}{4}$
5. $\frac{11}{200}$

Lesson 3.3, page 22
1. 27.4%
2. 0.587
3. 0.652
4. 0.63
5. 36.5%

Lesson 3.4, page 23
1. 25
2. 35
3. 8%
4. 40%
5. 20

Lesson 3.5, page 24
1. $67.50
2. $629.10
3. $6\frac{1}{2}$%
4. $2,450
5. 5

Lesson 3.6, page 25
1. $562.43
2. $508.82
3. $535.93
4. $562.75
5. $506.60

Posttest, page 26
1. 0.14 and $\frac{7}{50}$
2. $64.20
3. 45%
4. $600
5. $1,800
6. $213.32

Chapter 4

Pretest, page 27
1. 257
2. 27
3. 116
4. 9
5. 12
6. 10, 2

Lesson 4.1, page 28
1. 3
2. 7
3. 3
4. 75
5. $\frac{3}{4}$

Lesson 4.2, page 29
1. 6
2. 8
3. 3
4. $3\frac{1}{2}$
5. 22

Grade 8 Answers

Lesson 4.3, page 30
1. 21
2. 56
3. 420
4. 1,800
5. $3\frac{1}{2}$

Lesson 4.4, page 31
1. 13, 7
2. 24, 1
3. 6, 3
4. 14
5. 6, 5

Lesson 4.5, page 32
1. 1, 10
2. 1
3. 5
4. 2, 45
5. 1, 30

Posttest, page 33
1. $4\frac{1}{2}$
2. 93
3. 2, 338
4. 203
5. 80, 3
6. 1, 52

Chapter 5

Pretest, page 34
1. 31.2
2. 0.0038
3. 11,000
4. 1.475
5. 0.00379
6. 50

Lesson 5.1, page 35
1. 21,097.5
2. 243
3. 2.2
4. 1.6
5. 12.5

Lesson 5.2, page 36
1. 0.03784
2. 9.46
3. 2,840
4. 397.2
5. 2.365

Lesson 5.3, page 37
1. 425
2. 255,000
3. 0.442
4. 625
5. 64

Posttest, page 38
1. 1,000
2. 4
3. 113,400
4. 57.31
5. 2,500,000
6. 7,500

Mid-Test Chapters 1–5

Mid-Test, page 39
1. 21,568
2. 3,726
3. $71.90
4. $10.30
5. 342
6. $\frac{1}{16}$

Mid-Test, page 40
1. 225
2. 150
3. 16
4. $1,666.25
5. $96.75
6. 15

Mid-Test, page 41
1. 0.15, $\frac{3}{20}$
2. $917.10
3. 16%
4. $199.92
5. $339.99
6. $1,040.60

Mid-Test, page 42
1. 81,600,000
2. 761
3. 12,000
4. 9,260
5. 15, 9
6. 52,411, 1

Grade 8 Answers

Chapter 6

Pretest, page 43
1. BMX
2. 4
3. 14
4. 72
5. 120°
6. 25%; 90°
7. 7
8. 8
9. 15

Pretest, page 44
1. 63°
2. 65°
3. 62.2°
4. 19°
5. $\frac{3}{8}$
6. $\frac{1}{4}$
7. $\frac{5}{8}$
8. 12;

eagle — oriole / blue jay / cardinal

bear — oriole / blue jay / cardinal

dog — oriole / blue jay / cardinal

mule — oriole / blue jay / cardinal

Lesson 6.1, page 45
1. 111
2. science fiction
3. 18
4. 23
5. 1

Lesson 6.2, page 46
1. the number of hours studied
2. 6
3. 14
4. 6–6.9
5. 9

Lesson 6.3, page 47
1. 26
2. 15
3. 28
4. 4
5. 82

Lesson 6.4, page 48
1. 24
2. $\frac{1}{3}$; 33.3%
3. 15%
4. 63
5. 126

Lesson 6.5, page 49
1. age and shoe size
2. positive
3. 30
4. Ages 17 to 19
5. People stop growing after a certain age and their shoe size remains the same.

Lesson 6.6, page 50
1. 183
2. 186
3. 186; 95
4. It wouldn't change.
5. The range changed the most. Last year's range is 35 points less than this year's range.

Lesson 6.7, page 51
1. $\frac{2}{5}$
2. $\frac{1}{3}$
3. $\frac{1}{5}$
4. $\frac{1}{15}$
5. 30
6. 22

Lesson 6.8, page 52
1. 28; 12
2. 9
3. 8.6
4. 12
5. 16

Lesson 6.9, page 53
1. 27
2. 12
3. 5
4. 21
5. 29 and 33

Grade 8 Answers

Lesson 6.10, page 54

1. 12; **Sneakers   Shirts   Pants**

2. 6;

3. 6;

4. 4;

5. 12;

Lesson 6.11, page 55

1. a 3-by-5 matrix
2. history
3. reading
4. science and geography
5. math and science

Lesson 6.12, page 56

1. $\frac{3}{16}$
2. $\frac{1}{4}$
3. $\frac{1}{2}$
4. $\frac{7}{16}$
5. $\frac{11}{16}$

Posttest, page 57

1. 14
2. 13
3. 41
4. 3
5. inches of rain
6. 7
7. 10
8. 15

Posttest, page 58

1. 26
2. 37.5
3. 35
4. green beans
5. peas
6. no
7. $\frac{1}{10}$
8. $\frac{1}{10}$
9. $\frac{1}{5}$
10. $\frac{2}{5}$
11. $\frac{1}{5}$
12. 20

Chapter 7

Pretest, page 59

1. parallel
2. line segment HG
3. $\overrightarrow{HE}$, $\overrightarrow{HA}$, and vertex H
4. $\overrightarrow{EC}$ and $\overrightarrow{EF}$
5. $\angle 2$, $\angle 4$, $\angle 6$, $\angle 8$
6. $\angle 1/\angle 3$, $\angle 2/\angle 4$, $\angle 5/\angle 7$, $\angle 8/\angle 6$
7. $\angle 3/\angle 5$, $\angle 4/\angle 6$
8. right

Pretest, page 60

1. right scalene triangle
2. $\angle FMY$
3. dilation
4. 40
5. 30

Grade 8 Answers

Lesson 7.1, page 61
1. point *T*
2. $\overrightarrow{SR}$ or $\overrightarrow{RS}$
3. $\overrightarrow{AS}$ or $\overrightarrow{SA}$
4.

5.

Lesson 7.2, page 62
1. $\overrightarrow{XY}$
2. ∠*UVW*, ∠*WVU*, ∠*V*
3.

4. ∠*GJM*, ∠*MJG*, ∠*J*
5.

Lesson 7.3, page 63
1. acute, 40°
2. obtuse, 110°
3. right, 90°
4. obtuse, 165°
5. acute, 15°

Lesson 7.4, page 64
1. ∠*NOP* and ∠*SOR*
2. supplementary
3. complementary
4. 60°
5. 150°

Lesson 7.5, page 65
1. West and Main
2. Oak
3. ∠1/∠2, ∠2/∠3, ∠3/∠4, ∠4/∠1, ∠7/∠8, ∠8/∠5, ∠5/∠6, ∠6/∠7
4. ∠2/∠6, ∠3/∠7
5. ∠1/∠5, ∠4/∠8

Lesson 7.6, page 66
1. obtuse
2. right
3. obtuse
4. acute
5. right

Lesson 7.7, page 67
1. scalene
2. equilateral
3. scalene
4. isosceles
5. isosceles

Lesson 7.8, page 68
1. 8
2. 54
3. 10
4. 5

Lesson 7.9, page 69
1. 5
2. 7
3. 12
4. 11
5. 8, 9, 8

Lesson 7.10, page 70
1. 15
2. 40
3. 8
4. 36.6
5. 23.9

Lesson 7.11, page 71
1. 12
2. 24, 18
3. 12
4. 28
5. 60

Lesson 7.12, page 72
1. *P*(2, −1), *Q*(4, −1), *R*(5, −4), *S*(3, −6)
2. *P*′(0, 5), *Q*′(2, 5), *R*′(3, 2), *S*′(1, 0)
3. Translation
4. 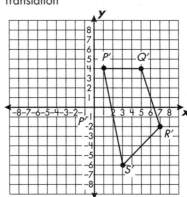 ; dilation
5. reflection

Posttest, page 73
1. $\overline{MS}$ and $\overline{LH}$
2. $\overline{CP}$
3. line segment $\overline{PC}$
4. ∠2, ∠3, ∠6, ∠7
5. ∠1/∠4, ∠5/∠8, ∠2/∠3, ∠6/∠7
6. ∠1, ∠4, ∠5, ∠8
7. ∠3/∠6, ∠4/∠5
8. ∠1/∠8, ∠2/∠7
9. 42°

Grade 8 Answers

Posttest, page 74

1. obtuse, scalene
2. 18 ft.
3. P(–4, 2), L(2, 2), A(2, –2), Y(–4, –2)
4. P'(–2, –2), L'(–2, 4), A'(2, 4), Y'(2, –2)
5. rotation

Chapter 8

Pretest, page 75

1. 1,728
2. 168
3. 120
4. 530.66
5. 81.64
6. 840

Pretest, page 76

1. 510
2. 504
3. 31.79
4. 10.6
5. SA = 282.6, V =314
6. SA = 144, V = 64

Lesson 8.1, page 77

1. 208
2. 288
3. 33
4. 60
5. 240

Lesson 8.2, page 78

1. 24
2. 15.75
3. square; 16
4. 112
5. 8.5

Lesson 8.3, page 79

1. 27
2. 112.5
3. 4.5
4. 625
5. 45

Lesson 8.4, page 80

1. 5.25, 32.97
2. 9, 28.26
3. 6
4. 3.75, 23.55
5. 6.5

Lesson 8.5, page 81

1. 17, 907.46
2. 46, 1,661.06
3. 36, 4,069.44
4. 16, 200.96
5. 44

Lesson 8.6, page 82

1. 1,394.76
2. 3,024
3. 55
4. 32
5. 9.5

Lesson 8.7, page 83

1. 264
2. 150
3. 1,936
4. 282
5. 1,776

Lesson 8.8, page 84

1. 2,160
2. 13,824
3. 16
4. 10,880
5. 6,480

Lesson 8.9, page 85

1. 1,256
2. 2,913.92
3. 282.6
4. 31.4
5. 13.4

Lesson 8.10, page 86

1. 251.2
2. 10.99
3. 150.72
4. 3
5. 113.04

Lesson 8.11, page 87

1. 301.44
2. 282.6
3. 351.68
4. 452.16
5. 1,808.64

Lesson 8.12, page 88

1. 200.96
2. 37.68
3. 527.52
4. 20.92
5. 2,659.58

Grade 8 Answers

Lesson 8.13, page 89
1. 11.44
2. 828
3. 7,776
4. 418.75
5. 9.2

Lesson 8.14, page 90
1. 2.42
2. 1,620
3. 2,880
4. 546.88
5. 1.73

Posttest, page 91
1. 9
2. 13
3. 1,800
4. 4,700
5. 7.065
6. 9.42
7. 339.12, 423.9

Posttest, page 92
8. 8,464
9. 51,072
10. 75.36
11. 37.68
12. 12.75
13. 3.75

Chapter 9

Pretest, page 93
1a. 7^5, 12^{-10}
1b. 1.952×10^3
1c. 0.00001974
2a. $6n + 9$
2b. $14 - n = 6$
3a. $a + b = b + a$
3b. $a(b + c) = ab + ac$
4a. $15n = 450$, \$30
4b. $2n + 14 = 32$, \$9

Lesson 9.1, page 94
1. 10^5
2. 5^6
3. 3^3
4. 2^{15}
5. 10^4

Lesson 9.2, page 95
1. 4^{-5}
2. 5^{-9}
3. 8^{-3}
4. 9^{10}
5. $10^2 \div 10^{-2}$

Lesson 9.3, page 96
1. 5.8×10^7
2. 778,500,000
3. 1.428×10^5
4. 7.46×10^{-2}
5. 0.834

Lesson 9.4, page 97
1. $3a$
2. $s + 8$
3. $2a > 20$
4. $2a \div 4 = 6$
5. $a - 3 = 15$

Lesson 9.5, page 98
1. 6
2. 32
3. 147
4. 21
5. She added before multiplying; 22

Lesson 9.6, page 99
1. $q \times p$
2. 0
3. Associative
4. 5
5. 1

Lesson 9.7, page 100
1. $(40 \times 30) + (2 \times 30) = 1,200 + 60 = 1,260$
2. $15a + 15b$
3. $(20 \times 10) + (20 \times 5) = 200 + 100 = 300$
4. $16 (30 + 20) = 16(50) = 800$
5. $10(t + s)$

Lesson 9.8, page 101
1. $n + 65 = 84$, \$19
2. $56 = x - 13$, \$69
3. $j + 9 = 64$, \$55
4. $p - 21 = 47$, \$68
5. $n + 35 = 56$, \$21

Lesson 9.9, page 102
1. $4f = 12$, 3 feet
2. $6 \times n = 30$, 5 pieces
3. $\frac{n}{5} = 4$, 20 feet
4. $\frac{n}{12} = 8$, 96 inches
5. $\frac{l}{3} = 8$, 24 feet

Lesson 9.10, page 103
1. \$1.50
2. 7
3. \$20
4. \$27
5. \$10

Grade 8 Answers

Lesson 9.11, page 104

1. T(–2, 4)
2. M(8, –2)
3.

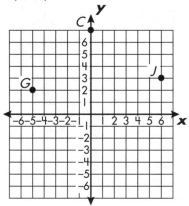

4. parallelogram

Lesson 9.12, page 105

1.

y
1
2
3
4
7

2.

x	y
–2	–11
–1	–8
0	–5
1	–2
2	1

3. $y = \frac{x^2}{3}$

4.

x	y
–6	12
–3	3
0	0
3	3
6	12

5. $y = x^2 + 1$

Lesson 9.13, page 106

1.

x	y
1	2
2	3
4	5
6	7

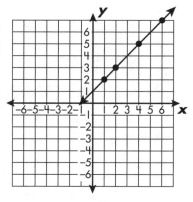

2.

x	y
1	–1
2	0
4	2
6	4

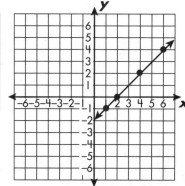

3.

x	y
1	–1
2	1
3	3
4	5

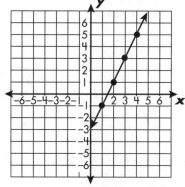

4.

x	y
1	1.5
2	2
4	3
6	4

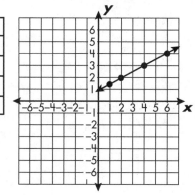

Grade 8 Answers

Posttest, page 107

1a. $9^3, 3^{-13}$
1b. $\frac{1}{16}$
1c. 3,400,000
2a. $n > 13$
2b. $17 + 11n = 50$
3. Associative Property of Addition
4a. $n - 5 = 14$, 19 years
4b. $3n + 12 = 42$, $10
5. 12

6.

x	y
−2	8
−1	6
0	4
1	2

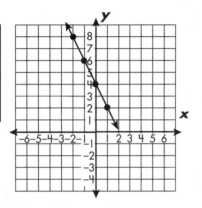

Final Test Chapters 1–9

Final Test, page 108

1. Equation: $72 + n = 87$, $n = \$15$
2. a) $44.70
   b) 15 gallons
   c) $97.35
3. 18 ounces
4. Equation: $2n - 3 = 21$, Bridget's score: 12 points, Opponent's score: 9 points
5. 6^2
6. a) 57 points
   b) Olivia

Final Test, page 109

1. 370.5, 77
2. 10, 1.33
3. 16.58, 5.02
4. $\frac{13}{20}$, 0.65, 65%
5. a) $12,000; $9,000
   b) $9,000; $9,500
6. $1,650

Final Test, page 110

1. 2^2
2. $672
3. $0.35
4. 13.5

5.

x	y
−1	−5
0	−3
1	−1
2	1

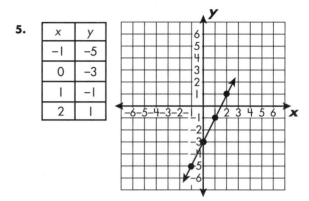

Final Test, page 111

1. acute isosceles
2. a) $A(3, 5), B(2, 1), C(4, 1)$
   b) $A'(-3, 5), B'(-4, 1), C'(-2, 1)$
   c) translation
3. 3.5
4. $\angle1/\angle3; \angle2/\angle4; \angle5/\angle7; \angle6/\angle8$
5. $\angle4/\angle6; \angle3/\angle5$
6. $\overrightarrow{YX}, \overrightarrow{YZ}$

Final Test, page 112

1. 20%
2. 19,580; 1.958×10^4
3. Equation: $\frac{9,880}{n} = 1,235$; $n = 8$ sections
4. $3\frac{11}{12}$; 235
5. $2n + 45$
6. a) 10,000–14,999
   b) 15

Final Test, page 113

1. 11,304; 376.8
2. 39
3. 0.20812
4. 1,392; 3,456
5. 42,000
6. 12;

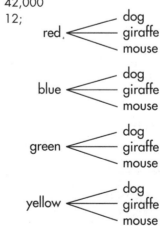